GARDENING
OFF THE
GROUND

Illustrations and cover art by Ron White

GARDENING OFF THE GROUND

Art C. Drysdale

J. M. Dent & Sons (Canada) Limited

Copyright © 1975
by J. M. DENT & SONS (CANADA) LIMITED

ISBN 0-460-91942-3

Printed in Canada

Contents

*A garden in containers many floors above the street
can be just as beautiful as a back garden.*

Introduction

If you have a balcony, this book is for you. Whether you live in a high-rise building, a town house, a condominium or co-operative, a low-rise, or even a flat in a house, you need no longer be excluded from the exciting new interest in gardening that has resulted from the ecological awakening and awareness of the 1970s.

The young couple who have just returned from their week's holiday in Honolulu do not have to live without the natural greenery they so much admired there, simply because they live in a tenth-floor apartment. It is not necessary for the retired couple to give away their entire cherished collection of roses and perennial flowers from their back garden simply because they are now moving to the fifteenth floor of a condominium.

The apartment or balcony garden is no longer a fantasy, and with the new concepts, new plants, and new products now being introduced, more people than ever before are finding satisfaction and pleasure in balcony gardening. Scientists have initiated programmes of breeding and selection, and have introduced new varieties of flowers and vegetables specifically for growing in containers on balconies. Many more plants of this kind are in the final testing and proving stages. Experts have perfected lighter-weight soil materials which are easier to handle and support plant growth better than most soils brought in from a suburban garden. Manufacturers have begun to produce long-lasting fertilizers in tablet form, capable of supplying the nutritional needs of a plant for six to nine months. Finally, the makers of rigid plastics and polyethylene are beginning to offer new container products – among them those featuring self-watering devices that allow plants to be left entirely without care for periods of up to a month.

It is the object of this book to make the reader aware of what is already possible for outdoor apartment gardens, as well as to suggest some experimental ideas that may expand gardening even further as an enjoyable and practical hobby for the millions of people who had once thought gardening on a balcony an impossibility.

Apartment Gardening
Is Different

1

On the arrival of spring, homeowners (even if they are not enthusiastic gardeners) traditionally buy a few plants for their front and back gardens either from a garden centre or from the local grocery store. When they get the plants home, it is a relatively simple matter to plunge them into the soil, water them, and wait to watch them grow.

However, for the apartment gardener, the approach must be different. Small plants in a box purchased in late May or early June from the neighbourhood supermarket or from a garden centre are probably left to grow in the box in which they came or, at best, planted in a window box containing not much more than 8 inches of soil. Such containers dry out very quickly, and if the plants are left in their original boxes they may die from drought during just one hot day in late June. Thus the balcony gardener is different from his ground-level counterpart in being immediately faced with discouraging results which tend to keep him from pursuing his hobby further.

Special Soil Mixes for Containers

Unlike ground-level gardeners, who always have soil easily available (if only a small patch of ground), balcony gardeners must depend on containers of varying sizes and shapes. The soil in these, because the volume is so small, needs changing or enriching periodically: from once each season to once every third season, depending on what is being grown. Keeping the containers filled is sometimes awkward, especially if ordinary garden soil – always heavy and usually messy – is used, and it has to be carried up and down stairs or in an elevator. New, packaged soil mixes in sealed plastic bags containing from two quarts to half a bushel help solve the dirt problem, while the weight problem can be alleviated by purchasing lightweight soil mixes. The Cornell lightweight soil mix, developed by Cornell University in the United States, can even be mixed in an apartment, once the ingredients have been purchased from a local garden supply store. The recipe is given on page 13.

Light Exposure

Perhaps the most obvious difference between gardening on a balcony and at ground level is exposure to the sun. Few apartments are fortunate enough to have balconies on more than one side of a building and, therefore, apartment gardeners must contend with a reduced amount of sunlight, no matter which direction the balcony faces. It is difficult to say which direction provides the best exposure, for that depends on what types and kinds of plants the apartment dweller hopes to grow. Probably, a balcony facing southwest comes closest to being the ideal. However, there are many plants that may be grown on balconies facing other directions, and suggestions for these are made in succeeding chapters.

Wind

To realize some of the effect of wind on balcony gardening as compared to ground-level gardening, we need only consider the wind-tunnel effects set up by any city's tall downtown buildings. Stronger winds are experienced at the upper floors of any building compared to those at the ground, and they indicate one of the problems encountered in trying to grow plants at high levels. Occasionally, the wind factor may dictate that large or tall plants in containers on a balcony be permanently staked or tied to a wall, or grown in heavier clay rather than in one of the lightweight growing media. However, the effect of wind may be minimized on most balconies in one or several ways – including the use of baffles and well-anchored trellises, the placement of the larger containers of plants, and particularly by the use of containers on casters. These easily moved containers enable a high-rise gardener to have no problem in moving his or her plant con-

If your balcony is windswept, you may help to prevent winds from blowing along its length by setting up wind baffles, though these should be used only on balconies that receive plenty of light at the front. The baffles, placed at the ends of the balcony, should be attached to the wall of the building by special masonry nails or plugs and to the railing, as shown. Climbing plants (perhaps vines) or potted plants attached by special clips may be used to cover the baffles.

tainers near the building during periods of high wind, and out against the railings when winds are low or the balcony is being used.

Window boxes planted with annual flowers of different varieties (depending on how much exposure there is to the sun) can usually withstand strong winds. Most annuals (particularly petunias, alyssum, snapdragons, verbena, marigolds, impatiens, and fibrous begonias) appreciate regular pruning that induces new branching, and strong winds cause little more harm to these plants than small broken stems. Good use may be made of such broken stems from flowering annuals for propagation of more plants, as discussed in Chapter 4, *Annuals: Flowers and Vines* (p. 37).

Gardening in Absentia

The other major difference between balcony and traditional home gardening is, more accurately, a basic difference between the gardeners themselves: apartment dwellers probably tend to be at home less than house dwellers. This difference is apparent in two ways.

First, in a high percentage of apartments, the occupants are absent during the daytime on weekdays. In houses, by contrast, a larger percentage are family units, with one member at home at least part of most days. Second, and probably mainly because of the nature of

10

apartments, apartment dwellers spend a good deal of their leisure time on weekends away from their homes. (Though of course people who live in houses also have cottages or campers and travel away on weekends.) But a fact of house ownership as opposed to apartment-home dwelling or even condominium-home ownership is the constant need to carry out regular maintenance chores or make changes to improve the owner's investment.

Nothing affects a garden as much as lack of regular and constant care. The balcony gardener's longer absences from home become even more significant when we consider that plants on balconies are always in a much smaller volume of soil than those planted in a ground-level garden. For this reason the soil dries out faster, and during hot periods small and medium-sized containers and window boxes must be watered at least once a day.

The answer to this problem is self-watering devices – either home inventions added to existing containers, or one of the several different types of commercial devices. The third alternative is to use some of the newly available self-watering containers. Through one, or a combination, of these ideas, balcony planters can be fixed so that watering need only be carried out once a week or even as infrequently as once a month.

The remainder of this book is really a detailed examination of the ways and means of achieving success in balcony gardening, or, in other words, of solving the problems that have been outlined in this chapter.

Fatten the Soil

2

An old proverb says, 'The master's footsteps fatten the soil.' The modern balcony gardener need not use his feet, just his head, in deciding what type of soil and fertilizer to use in his containers, and whether or not he should maintain a compost pile.

Gardening in Soil

In the previous chapter I suggested that balcony gardeners use pre-packaged soil mixes rather than ordinary garden soils, which are heavy and awkward to handle as well as being dirty or at least messy. If you need a large amount of planting medium, you may find it worthwhile to make your own Cornell mix. Most of the materials you will require are available at well-stocked garden and plant supply centres. Potassium nitrate (known as saltpetre) can be obtained from drugstores. If you decide to make your own mix, following the recipe given here, it is important that you do not alter the amounts or substitute alternative ingredients, even though a salesman who does not happen to handle a certain ingredient tells you that his substitute is just as good.

The mix may be put together in batches – on the kitchen table, outdoors, or perhaps even on the balcony floor. However, since you should be attempting to achieve a sterilized mix, I recommend that before you begin you use javel water to wipe down the entire mixing area and to clean the mixing utensils.

 1 bushel shredded peat moss
 1 bushel horticultural vermiculite (No. 4 is the best size of
   particle)
10 level tablespoons ground limestone
 5 level tablespoons potassium nitrate
   (known as saltpetre at your drugstore)
 1 teaspoon chelated iron
 1 gallon warm water

Mix all the ingredients thoroughly together.
If you find you have mixed more than you need, store the
excess in a plastic bag.

Fertilizers – A Simple Basic Course

Plants, like human beings, need certain nutrients in order to thrive.
The three basic elements used by plants are nitrogen, phosphorus,
and potassium (or potash). By law, the containers of all fertilizers sold
in Canada and the United States must show on the front the percen-
tages contained of each of these three elements. For example, a fertilizer with the ratio 4-12-8 on the container has 4 per cent nitrogen, 12
per cent phosphorus (in the form of phosphate), and 8 per cent
potash. The remainder of the material in the container comprises the
carrier on which those active ingredients are based, certain trace elements (such as sulphur) also used by the plants, and inert ingredients
(those without any active property) to make the product easier to
handle.
   The nitrogen, phosphate, and potash are each useful to plants for
different purposes, and once you understand these it will be relatively
simple for you to choose the correct ratio for any particular plant.
Nitrogen encourages the growth of foliage – the more nitrogen that is
available to a plant, the more luxuriant will be its foliage. Therefore,
foliage plants such as philodendron should be given a fertilizer high in
nitrogen – for example, 25-15-20. Phosphate induces flower and fruit
development and helps provide a strong and healthy root system.
Thus, for flowering plants or for vegetables such as tomatoes, you
should use a fertilizer such as 15-30-15 or the long-lasting 7-40-6
tablets now available that need only be mixed into the soil when the

container is planted in order to feed the plants for the entire season. Potash, the third of the three major elements, fosters disease resistance and tissue hardiness in plants, and works along with the other two to keep plants healthy.

Throughout this book I suggest the use of liquid fertilizers (the ones that come in crystalline form ready to be dissolved in water) because they are so much easier to apply than the granular type. Most liquid fertilizers are more expensive than their granular counterparts, since all the chemicals they contain are instantly soluble, and more highly refined. The soluble fertilizers are ideal for fertilizing the comparatively small quantities of soil in your containers. Plants will absorb a small part of their needs instantly through the foliage, and the remainder more slowly through the roots after the plant food has dripped down from the leaves and soaked into the soil.

There are only a few other facts about fertilizers that the balcony gardener need know. First, a number of all-purpose liquid fertilizers are available, usually with an analysis 20-20-20. These may be used on any plant, though you will probably find that they are not quite as effective as the specific formulations I have suggested earlier in this section.

You should not give fertilizer of any kind to a dry or wilting plant; its appearance indicates that it is in very poor condition, and the fertilizer may prove to be too much of a shock. First try to return the plant to normal by watering it, then apply the fertilizer. Also, to avoid causing shock, do not apply liquid fertilizer to the foliage of container plants while they are in direct and hot sun; wait until they are in the shade or, if you are using movable containers, move them.

Finally, never mix more than the recommended amount of fertilizer to the gallon or quart of water. If you have reason to believe that your plants need additional fertilizer, perhaps because they have not received any for six or eight weeks, just water them for longer than usual with the regular strength fertilizer solution, or at more frequent intervals.

A Balcony Compost Pile

With the increased emphasis on recycling garbage has come a rekindled interest on the part of ground level gardeners in making compost. High-rise gardeners, too, can have compost 'piles' that will not be objectionable to their neighbours. The compost container may simply be a large plastic garbage pail, with an 8- to 10-inch layer of soil at the bottom. Into this container you may throw all your unwrapped kitchen wastes, and even the contents of your vacuum-cleaner bag when you empty it.

At first you will need only one garbage can. But when it is full of kitchen wastes, dead annuals, and material pruned from your plants, put it aside for a year and start a second one. Each spring, use the compost from the can that has been allowed to stand for at least a year, whose contents have been broken down by bacterial action. Should you find some pieces not completely broken down when you empty out the material from the 'finished' container, just return them to your current container and give them another year to disintegrate.

As your current compost 'pile' builds up, you should scatter a few inches of good garden loam (obtained perhaps from a friendly ground-level gardener) and an ounce of a general granular fertilizer (7-7-7, for example) on top of the compost once a month or so, before you add more waste material. The loam will add bacteria to the pile. A further way of speeding up bacterial action is to churn the material in the garbage can every month. 'Compost makers', bacterial additives sold to hasten the breakdown of material in compost piles, may also be added; however, if a layer of soil and some fertilizer is added every 6 to 8 inches, and the pile is churned regularly, break-down should occur rapidly without additives.

COMPOSTING MATERIAL
SOIL 1½"
COMPOSTING MATERIAL 6"
SOIL 1½"
COMPOSTING MATERIAL 6"
SOIL 8"

A plastic garbage pail makes an ideal compost 'pile': two are even better. They may be kept under a table or shelf on which plant containers, troughs, or flower boxes are arranged. If hanging plants such as German ivy are grown in these, the pails will be partially screened from view.

Methods of Gardening on a Balcony

Initially, the apartment dweller may think only in terms of long, narrow window boxes attached to outside railings as his potential balcony garden. While such boxes do beautify both the individual apartment balcony and the building as a whole, other forms of planting are not merely possible; they can be highly successful.

No Need to Copy the Europeans

Balconies lined with plants, especially geraniums, are one of the features that give the streets of many European cities their undoubted charm. While our Canadian homes and cities may be improved by using plants in the European way, we should also try to use the alternative methods and styles that are suited to our own environment. We are able to adopt additional methods of balcony planting because our balconies are generally much larger (especially wider) than the European ones. This extra width should allow enough space for plantings that will create garden environments more like the ones normally found at ground level. In this chapter we shall explore various types of plantings – and you may want to use combinations of these for your own balcony garden.

Flower Boxes on the Railing

Flower boxes are hardly a new planting device even in Canada. However, the variety of sizes and types now available to apartment dwellers not only makes a continuous garden along a balcony rail possible, but also brings such an arrangement within the reach of even a modest budget. When shopping for window boxes or, more properly speaking, balcony railing boxes, start early in the season and visit not only department stores but the larger hardware outlets, garden centres, and discount stores. Even if you live in the inner core of a city, try to go and see what is available at plazas and centres in the suburbs as well as in the downtown stores near your building.

Before making your final selection, remember to consider the method of hanging, the size, design, material, price, and colour – in that order. Colour is the least important consideration because the outside of the box may soon be covered by hanging plants such as ivy, cascading petunias, and spider plants. However, remember that dark-coloured containers dry out much faster than the light-coloured ones. The method of hanging is the prime consideration in purchasing a balcony railing box. If it cannot easily be mounted on your railing or balcony enclosure, you could well find yourself paying out twice as much as the original investment in time and money before it is satisfactorily mounted.

Some high-rise buildings require that flower boxes on balcony railings be mounted on the *inside* of the railing, rather than on the outside. Not only is this method a safety measure to prevent the boxes from falling; it also stops dirty water from dripping onto the balconies beneath if the plants are over-watered or when there are rainstorms. If your management does not regulate balcony railing boxes in this way, you may wish to hang the boxes on the outside, anchoring them securely and being careful when watering. Boxes on the outside of railings not only give more space on the balcony itself, but give a more colourful view to people in the streets below or in nearby apartments and buildings.

The size of your window box is important; some are so small that the volume of soil they hold won't retain moisture for more than a day. Make sure that the inside depth is at least 8 inches, and the width (at the top of the box) 10 inches. In planting a box of this size, if you put an inch of large drainage material at the bottom and then fill it with soil reaching to an inch from the top of the box to facilitate watering, there will then be a soil depth of only 6 inches – and that is considered to be the minimum.

There are three main features to consider in the design of your flower box. It may or may not have drainage holes; it may be slope-

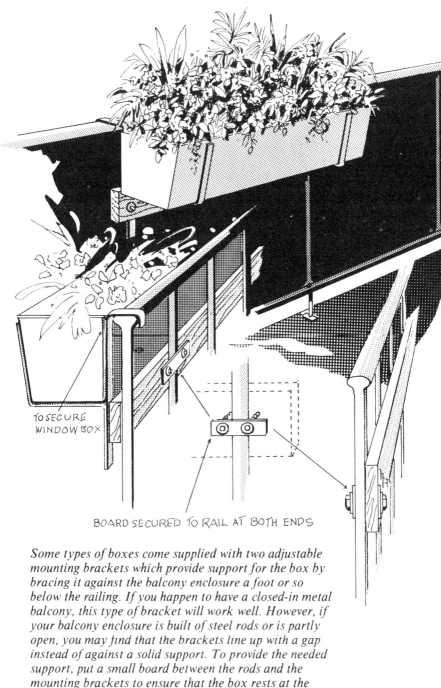

TO SECURE
WINDOW BOX

BOARD SECURED TO RAIL AT BOTH ENDS

*Some types of boxes come supplied with two adjustable
mounting brackets which provide support for the box by
bracing it against the balcony enclosure a foot or so
below the railing. If you happen to have a closed-in metal
balcony, this type of bracket will work well. However, if
your balcony enclosure is built of steel rods or is partly
open, you may find that the brackets line up with a gap
instead of against a solid support. To provide the needed
support, put a small board between the rods and the
mounting brackets to ensure that the box rests at the
correct angle.*

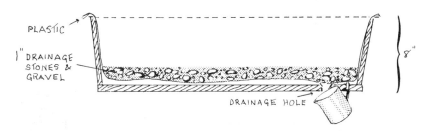

PLASTIC

1" DRAINAGE STONES & GRAVEL

8"

DRAINAGE HOLE

If you find it absolutely necessary to prevent your window boxes from dripping even very slightly, line them with a sheet of heavy plastic. Punch a hole in a front corner of the sheet and make a hole in the window box itself. Put a small tin underneath to catch the drips.

sided (the top wider than the bottom) or straight-sided; it may or may not be lined with long-lasting material.

If drainage holes are included, the box will definitely drip water after heavy rainstorms or if too much water is applied artificially. Although this drainage is a necessity for the plants, water dripping from boxes that are hung on the outside of the railing may be a nuisance, particularly to apartments below yours. Boxes without holes should be made either of plastic or fiberglas, or if they are made of wood should be lined with galvanized metal to prevent them from rotting. When you are planting boxes without drainage holes, be certain to include about an inch of broken clay flower pots, large stones or gravel, or any other chunky rubble to provide drainage. In addition, add a small amount of charcoal – most important to keep the soil from becoming sour. If the drainage material is extremely coarse, the soil on top may easily fall through it and fill the open spaces. To avoid that, place a piece of old wire screening, cheesecloth, or other porous material immediately above the drainage material to keep the soil out of the needed air space. It is important that boxes exposed to rainfall, particularly those on railings, be equipped with drainage holes, since one heavy rainstorm could waterlog the soil and thus kill the plants.

Generally speaking, slope-sided boxes are better than straight-sided, since less soil is required to achieve the same depth of soil and width of planting area at the top. Drainage is also more satisfactory in boxes with one or two slanting sides.

Wooden boxes still remain the most popular, particularly those of long-lasting wood such as red cedar. They are attractive, suit almost any décor, and, because they are now mass-produced, are not overly

19

expensive. Boxes made of various rigid plastics and of fiberglas are also available. These are light in weight and easier to handle than the wooden ones, but often require a greater number of supporting brackets to prevent stress or breakage, which may put up the cost of the complete unit.

In planning to purchase plastic or fiberglas boxes of a specific colour, remember that if these are exposed to full sun (west or south exposure) for a full season they may well fade to an unattractive pastel. Again, try to use light-coloured boxes, which will keep the soil cooler on hot days.

While the soil may be left in most flower boxes over winter without causing damage, remember that at least half the previous year's soil should be removed each spring and replaced with fresh soil. This soil replenishment should be carried out even if you intend to fertilize the plants throughout the growing season. There is a tendency for the organic content of soil in a small box to be washed to the bottom, and for the soil to build up harmful acid deposits if it is not replenished regularly, though charcoal added to the drainage material does help to prevent the acid deposits.

Flower Boxes on the Building

Although in the preceding discussion on flower boxes I have dealt strictly with balcony railing boxes, it may be desirable to mount boxes directly on the face of the building. On buildings with waist-level windows facing the balcony, this type of installation may be possible by mounting traditional window boxes on sills or by installing mounting brackets on the face of the building itself (see the comments on diamond drilling in the section about Hanging Baskets, p. 28). Alternatively, wood- or plastic-backed hooks may be attached to concrete walls with strong epoxy resin glue, and the window boxes hung from those.

The one point of difference to remember between boxes on the railing and those against the building is the exposure to light. On any balcony, regardless of the way it faces, there will almost certainly be less light for plant growth back against the building than out on the railing. This difference simply means that if a lack of light (for example, on a balcony facing north or east) is a concern, then the extra little bit of daily sunlight received by plants at the railing may be just the amount to mean the difference between success and mediocrity.

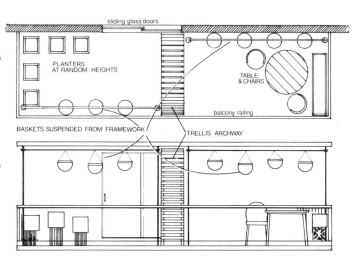

sliding glass doors

PLANTERS
AT RANDOM HEIGHTS

TABLE
& CHAIRS

balcony railing

BASKETS SUSPENDED FROM FRAMEWORK

TRELLIS ARCHWAY

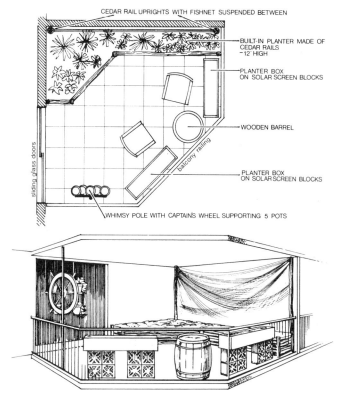

CEDAR RAIL UPRIGHTS WITH FISHNET SUSPENDED BETWEEN

BUILT-IN PLANTER MADE OF
CEDAR RAILS
~12' HIGH

PLANTER BOX
ON SOLAR SCREEN BLOCKS

WOODEN BARREL

balcony railing

sliding glass doors

PLANTER BOX
ON SOLAR SCREEN BLOCKS

WHIMSY POLE WITH CAPTAIN'S WHEEL SUPPORTING 5 POTS

*Whatever the shape and size of your balcony, you
can plan a garden to suit it – and yourself.*

Balcony Containers

The other popular form of instant landscaping on a balcony, patio pots or containers, can be set on the balcony floor. These containers come in various forms and shapes, and when deciding which ones to buy you should consider in this order: weight (or portability), durability, size, design, price, and colour. As with balcony railing boxes, colour is a minor concern, for trailing plants may easily be trained to cover the outsides and, in fact, make containers look far more natural. Prices vary, but the amount you pay could depend as much on where you shop as on the type of container you choose.

The first two factors – weight (or portability) and durability – are both directly dependent on the materials used in manufacture. Some of the earliest containers, produced in the late 1950s, were made of asbestos and cement. While they were fairly light in weight and an attractive off-white colour, they tended to break down (partially disintegrate) if left outside during the winter. Since that time, many new containers have been marketed, and these are now available in concrete (stable but heavy), plastic and fiberglas (lightweight and economical), wood (relatively light, with a natural appearance), and asbestos with medusa cement (white, medium weight, suited to modern architecture).

Like the balcony railing boxes, plastic or fiberglas containers may fade in full sun and some may not last long; but they should not be overlooked since they are quite economical. Concrete containers, or the larger asbestos-cement containers once they have been filled with soil, will be difficult to move around unless you put them on casters. Portability is an advantage, for it not only allows you to move the containers so that they get a maximum of sun, but enables you to make better use of your balcony for different purposes – for example, when you move the plants aside for parties.

Most of the containers placed on the balcony floor are larger than the railing containers, and they should be deeper. A minimum depth of 12 inches, with outside dimensions of 36 inches (circumference of a circular container or permimeter of a rectangular one) is reasonable. The maximum size should be dictated only by cost and by the size of the balcony and freight elevator. Design includes the same factors as those noted for railing boxes, and if there are no drainage holes you will need a layer of drainage material at the bottom. It is also highly recommended that you change at least a third of the soil each year.

The newest concept in balcony planters is a bag of peat moss and nutrients now being sold ready for planting with either seeds or started plants. The 2 by 3 feet plastic bag, weighing about twelve pounds, contains all the needed plant nutrients for up to eight weeks of growth; after that time, additional fertilizers will be required. The bag may be retained for a second season or discarded.

Self-Watering Containers

For people who cannot give their balcony gardens constant attention, self-watering containers are invaluable. These containers are being manufactured commercially, and as the demand for them grows, they will doubtless be produced in greater quantities and in a wider variety of designs. While many people may choose to buy the convenience of self-watering containers, others may still demand the convenience of self-watering but would rather not spend their money in this way, preferring instead to devise their own methods. Any enthusiastic handyman, once he has examined a self-watering container, should be able to build one to suit his own needs.

Self-watering containers work in a simple way: water from a built-in reservoir holding a three- to four-weeks' supply is conducted into the soil through a wick, the amount of wick increasing in proportion to the volume of soil held by the container. When the time comes to put the self-watering container into operation, it is important that the reservoir be filled to the top, and not filled again until the top two inches of soil are dry. The reservoir should then be refilled to the top and the water level gradually allowed to go down, as before. If a self-watering container is planted with small plants, it may be necessary to water it from the top for about ten days until the wick system is able to keep all the soil moist.

Recently, a further refinement of self-watering containers has been marketed: containers which hook up to the central water system of a home, and by means of a float and valve automatically regulate the flow of water into the containers' reservoirs in much the same way that automatic icemakers draw on house water systems to replenish ice cubes as they are used up. Some homemade systems of this kind are already in use.

The simplest self-watering container – the hanging flowerpot – can be constructed by almost any apartment dweller. Punch a hole in the centre of a lid from a screw-topped jar, and attach the lid to the

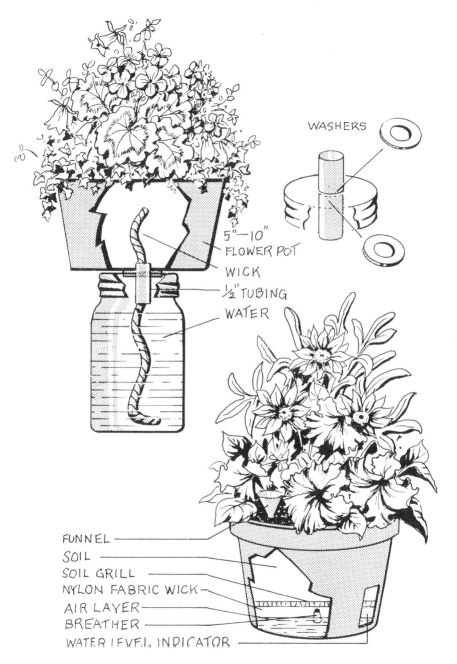

WASHERS

5"—10"
FLOWER POT
WICK
1/2" TUBING
WATER

FUNNEL
SOIL
SOIL GRILL
NYLON FABRIC WICK
AIR LAYER
BREATHER
WATER LEVEL INDICATOR

Whether your self-watering container is a homemade product (top) or commercially manufactured (below), the way it works is essentially the same.

bottom of a large pot by using an outside threaded piece of pipe half an inch in diameter (similar to the pipe used in attaching lamp sockets to their bases) and two half-inch nuts. If the hole in the base of the pot is considerably larger than your half-inch pipe, you will also need two large washers. Obtain a nylon wick from a garden supply store (or use strips from discarded nylon stockings) and insert it through the pipe into the soil of the flowerpot to about a third the depth of the pot. Cut the other end of the wick so that it is a little longer than the depth of the jar, which can now be screwed back into its lid. And there's your hanging flowerpot with its own attached reservoir that may be refilled as needed by unscrewing the jar. If you plant cascading plants such as petunias and ivy around the edge of the pot, they will hang down and soon cover the reservoir. Of course you may wish to devise your own unique self-watering container, using some of the attractive and inexpensive materials available.

Climbing Vines

Obviously, it's not much use having a movable container if you are going to grow climbing vines in it. For these, use instead almost any type of patio or balcony planter. The planter should be placed close to the railing and, if there are supports going up from the railing to the balcony ceiling, you have a ready-prepared trellis. If there are no such supports, a simple trellis of any style may be secured to the railing and will provide support for one or several vines. Even more economically, you could attach a single bamboo pole to the railing and tie twine to it at various levels. These pieces of twine can then be run down and tied to the railing. Pole and twine thus provide a tall mast and supporting lines on which fast-growing vines will give shade for part of the balcony. If you wish to try a vine on a trellis placed against the building wall, remember that there is less light in this position. In chapters 4 and 7 I shall make some suggestions for trying different varieties of vines.

Planters Nearer Eye Level

Wrought iron or other types of plant stands are now available for many of the planters that would otherwise be useful only on the balcony floor. These stands bring the colour (and sometimes the fragrance) of the plants much closer to eye level. While this height is not natural in a garden, where except for terraces all plants grow at ground level, it does make up for the lack of some of the taller-growing flowers and shrubs that cannot easily be grown on a balcony. Elevated containers also give space for more plants in the small area available on balconies, and allow you to concentrate your gardening in one corner of your balcony if you wish. When you purchase a container, check to see whether there is a stand that fits it (or that could be purchased later) if you would like some of your garden raised to waist level.

Containers at No Cost or Low Cost

Plant containers such as I have been discussing have one factor in common that could deter some apartment dwellers from starting a small garden: the containers all cost money. But those on austerity budgets need not despair; instead they should be alert – for there are many types of containers available that cost probably no more than going to get them.

First and foremost among the free plant containers are your own discards. Do not throw anything out without considering its potential as a balcony container: the largest fruit, vegetable, and juice cans, old

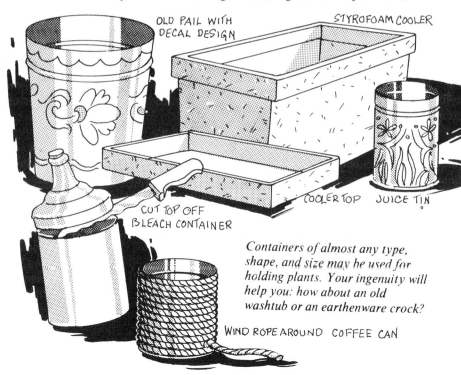

OLD PAIL WITH DECAL DESIGN

STYROFOAM COOLER

COOLER TOP   JUICE TIN

CUT TOP OFF
BLEACH CONTAINER

Containers of almost any type, shape, and size may be used for holding plants. Your ingenuity will help you: how about an old washtub or an earthenware crock?

WIND ROPE AROUND COFFEE CAN

Old-style wicker bicycle baskets (the type attached to the handlebars), which are semi-circular in shape and have one flat side, make ideal containers not only for the insides of railings but also for the end walls of balconies. Set plants in their pots inside them, or line them with plastic sheeting and treat them in the same way as window boxes. Annuals such as dwarf marigolds and snapdragons, lobelia, and sweet alyssum are especially suitable for these baskets.

pails of any sort (try a bakery), discarded portable styrofoam pop coolers, small old garbage cans, and food service jam tins. And ask your friends to keep their eyes open for containers like these. A little paint on the outside and perhaps a lining of plastic is all that is needed to complete a useful recycling.

A second way of obtaining cheap containers is to use new articles originally intended for a different purpose. Most of the items mentioned in the previous paragraph can be bought quite reasonably and, in addition to those, there are indoor and outdoor plastic garbage pails, damaged but new roasting pans and similar kitchen equipment, and plastic-lattice clothes baskets. By lining these baskets with a double sheet of polyethylene (2 mill) you will have attractive and large plant containers.

From small fruit and meat stores nearly-new bushel baskets may sometimes be available at the store owner's cost, or new ones may be obtained from some department stores. Provided that they are new or fairly new, wooden bushel baskets make excellent plant containers, preferably lined with plastic to prevent them from rotting prematurely. Wicker or plastic bicycle baskets – or rather half-baskets – are quite suitable for use on end walls, but plant them with bushy annuals, for the tall ones will lean too much towards the light.

You may want to include some small holes in the bottoms of these homemade containers to allow excess water to run out. Or you may prefer to treat them in the same manner as new containers without drainage holes – by putting a one-inch (or more) layer of large stones or similar material at the bottom, before filling them with soil mix, but be sure they are not exposed to heavy rainfalls.

Hanging Baskets

Until recently an almost forgotten vogue, hanging baskets are now increasing in popularity. Today they are seen quite commonly on the verandas of older houses and on the porches and decks of new subdivision homes. They have also been made popular by various parks departments, probably first on a large scale in Canada by the city of Victoria, British Columbia, through their use along main shopping streets.

But hanging baskets have been slow to catch on with apartment dwellers mainly because, in most apartments, there is literally no

The hanging flower baskets in Victoria, B.C., are among the best (and most photographed) examples of this kind of floral decoration in Canada.

If your neighbour above has no objection, you might suspend your hanging baskets from the railings of the balcony immediately above yours. For strength and safety, use heavy clothesline wire (plastic coated) or 14-gauge electrical wire.

place from which to hang them. The most up-to-date and usual method of constructing balconies for both low- and high-rise buildings today is to use poured concrete, but the inhabitants find it almost impossible to suspend flower baskets from solid concrete. One solution, practised by a few avid apartment gardeners, has been to obtain permission from their neighbour immediately above to suspend two or three wires from the base of the railing at the point where it is embedded in the concrete floor. The wires, allowed to hang down below the neighbour's floor for two or three feet, could have the hanging baskets attached to the ends. This procedure may still be followed where an apartment dweller is lucky enough to find a co-operative neighbour above. However, an alternative exists. Most management companies will now undertake to have a specialist use a diamond drill on the balcony ceilings of tenants wishing to instal flower baskets. Provided that enough tenants in any one complex of buildings request this service at the same time, the cost to each should not be great.

The flower baskets, in addition to being suspended from the balcony ceiling near the railing (where the light is brightest), may also be hung from special wrought-iron brackets installed on the wall of the building. This position is really only worth considering if you have a south, west, or southwesterly exposure. Once again, a diamond drill would be necessary.

Flower baskets are available each May and June already planted, but if you wish to save a little money you may purchase the makings yourself. You will need baskets (now usually plastic) complete with hanging chains, a small amount of sphagnum moss (not peat moss) to line them in order to retain the moisture, some potting soil (or good garden loam obtained from a ground-level gardener), and a selection of plants – some details about these are given in the next chapter. Many gardeners like to line hanging baskets with a piece of plastic containing only one drainage hole in order to keep water drips to a minimum, but some still prefer to have the sphagnum moss touching the plastic-mesh basket and water only sparingly to prevent excessive dripping.

Johnny Poles

Most people usually think of Johnny poles as those utilitarian, chrome, spring-loaded poles used in bathrooms. But, if you are a

gardener, put that usual thought right out of your mind. At least one Canadian manufacturer now makes spring-loaded poles with a dull black finish which hold an array of matching brackets. The brackets hold from three to eight beautifully hand-crafted natural clay and painted pots of various sizes and designs. A unit such as this, while rather more expensive than one or two plastic containers on the balcony floor, has two distinct advantages: first, it provides colour on the balcony literally from floor to ceiling, and second, it may be brought into the apartment for the winter season and the containers filled with suitable indoor plants. Used inside as well as out, the pole and planters double your investment! Made of natural clay and without a drainage hole, these planters are ideal for inside use, for if you take care to control the watering, any excess water will evaporate from the outside of the pot and there will be no dripping.

Floor Gardens

Another form of apartment gardening not well known in Canada is something I call *floor gardening*. Basically, it consists of turning part of the balcony, preferably the sunniest area, into a small garden on top of the concrete. Using a few pieces of rough-grade lumber (1 by 8 or 1 by 10-inch), which can be new or used, board off either a triangular or a rectangular section at one end of the balcony. If you have an extra-wide balcony, you might use additional lumber to make a garden along the front of the balcony and leave the sitting area across the length adjacent to the building. It might be well to check whether your building management has established any weight restrictions.

Boards should be put along all sides of the floor garden, including the railing side, since there is almost always an opening between the

Your Johnny pole may be set up outside on the balcony from June to September, and inside the apartment from October to May. Provided that some drainage material, such as gravel, is put at the bottom of the natural clay containers, they may be filled directly with soil. Because there is so much less light inside most apartments than out on the balcony, the plants you select for your Johnny pole when it is indoors should be only those that need very little light, such as spider plant, fibrous begonias, pothos, and grape ivy.

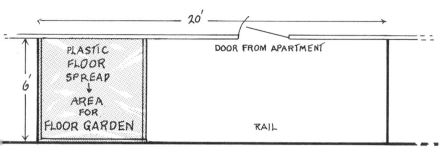

<------ 20' ------>

PLASTIC FLOOR SPREAD ↓ AREA FOR FLOOR GARDEN

6'

DOOR FROM APARTMENT

RAIL

Choose the far end of your balcony for your floor garden, and remember that unless you have a particularly large balcony, it is best not to restrict your use of the space by taking up more than a third of the total area for the garden.

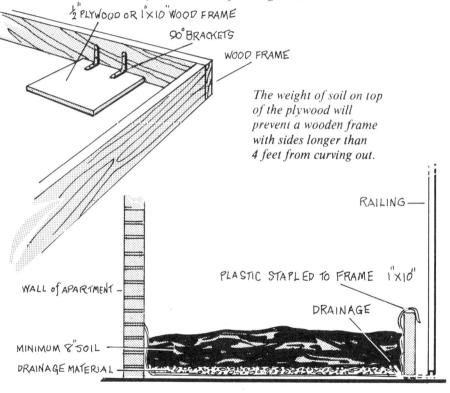

½" PLYWOOD OR 1"X10" WOOD FRAME

90° BRACKETS

WOOD FRAME

The weight of soil on top of the plywood will prevent a wooden frame with sides longer than 4 feet from curving out.

RAILING—

PLASTIC STAPLED TO FRAME 1"X10"

WALL of APARTMENT—

DRAINAGE

MINIMUM 8" SOIL

DRAINAGE MATERIAL

A section through a floor garden. Note especially the lining (polyethylene sheeting), the channel for drainage (necessary if the balcony is at all subject to downpours of rain), and the soil towards the centre of the garden mounded in order to get a greater depth than is dictated by the width of the side supports.

bottom of the railing and the concrete floor. A support should be mounted in the middle of each board over 4 feet long, to prevent it from bowing out or buckling. Ninety-degree metal brackets attached to another flat board along the floor should suffice.

Once the form for the floor garden has been made, it should be lined with sheet polyethylene (2 mill is best) which is usually available in paint supply stores for use as drop sheets. The lining should be attached with double-sided carpet tape or stapled to the top of the plank sides to prevent constant moisture from dripping over the edge of the balcony. The garden is now ready for drainage material. Use round beach stones or pebbles rather than sharp-edged gravel, which might cut through the polyethylene. Put in about an inch of the drainage material mixed with chunks of charcoal – about a quarter of a bag of charcoal per square yard of floor garden. The charcoal will keep the soil from taking on a sour odour. If the floor garden area is at all likely to be soaked by rainfall, you should allow for drainage by cutting holes in the polyethylene at the railing side.

On top of the drainage material, spread a well-mixed combination of about a third each of peat moss, loam, and sand. Be sure the peat moss is moist before you include it. Though slightly more expensive, loose, bagged peat moss, which has already been dampened, is much easier to use than the extremely dry baled type.

As an alternative to the peat moss, loam, and sand, you might prefer to use either a prepared lightweight soil mix available from garden supply stores, or a large batch of Cornell mix; see p.13 for the recipe. Charcoal should also be added to the soil mix, to prevent the soil from souring.

When you have put the soil mix into your floor garden, be sure to tramp it down well with your feet. After the soil has been tramped, its final level should be about half an inch below the top of the outside retaining boards, but in the centre of the garden the soil level may be mounded from 3 to 6 inches higher to accommodate some of the larger plants that we shall talk about in Chapter 6 (p. 71).

Multi-level Floor Gardens

A further refinement of the floor garden on larger balconies is possible by raising the garden and making several different planting areas on varying levels. Different heights are probably best achieved by using large prepared beams from the demolition of older buildings.

Multi-level floor gardens present a wide variety of planting opportunities, since the depths of soil at the back may reach 2 feet or more – sufficient for larger shrubs and even small trees.

The appearance of old beams is far more attractive even than new lumber that has been stained.

The beams may be installed in almost any pattern, but you should make certain that there are no tiny, nuisance planting pockets (with sides less than 8 inches long) and that a few of the larger pockets are at least 18 inches deep, so that some of the more permanent plants may be grown.

While a multi-level floor garden will cost considerably more to build than a single-level garden (in terms particularly of labour, but also of material) neither garden need be a permanent fixture. Without much difficulty both types of garden can be dismantled and reassembled in a different pattern, or taken to a new location and rebuilt to suit another balcony.

In both single- and multi-level floor gardens, the soil mix may only need to be changed or partly replenished every third year, depending on the amount of charcoal that was added and how the garden is watered and fertilized. Over-watering or heavy applications of fertilizer will result in a build-up of harmful salts that can only be corrected by changing all or part of the soil, or by watering heavily in the early spring.

A Balcony Greenhouse

While discussing the more elaborate gardens possible on a balcony, it is worthwhile to consider the feasibility of a balcony greenhouse. The installation of a greenhouse on an apartment balcony is obviously a feature that will interest only a minority of apartment dwellers; nevertheless, as costs come down, or remain constant, for many more keen gardeners the idea is bound to become more than just a dream.

Today, it seems that the main deterrent to balcony greenhouses is the restriction imposed, or that balcony gardeners imagine is imposed, by the owners – especially management companies – of large apartment complexes. Municipal authorities often advise management companies that because a greenhouse comprises an extra room, **the property** taxes will increase. Little or no such problem

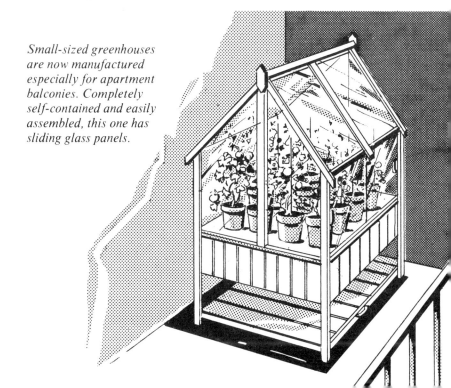

Small-sized greenhouses are now manufactured especially for apartment balconies. Completely self-contained and easily assembled, this one has sliding glass panels.

apparently exists for condominium owners; in fact, a greenhouse on a balcony will raise the selling value of a condominium home, which could offset any small increase in taxes.

When you are considering setting up a greenhouse on your balcony, you should be aware that it is likely to be a success only if your balcony faces south or southwest. Apartment or condominium dwellers wishing to create an enlarged growing area, but who face north, east, or due west, would be better advised to consider a plant room with fluorescent and other artificial lighting.

The best type of greenhouse for a balcony is a lean-to, using the wall of the apartment building on which to lean the structure. Ideally it should be the size of the balcony itself, but if the balcony is extremely large (perhaps 8 by 20 feet) a greenhouse of 8 by 10 feet could be installed at one end. It would be entered through the door to the apartment, and another single, hinged door could be placed in the end wall of the greenhouse to give access to the remaining part of the balcony.

A number of easily assembled greenhouses are currently available on the Canadian market: they are of aluminum or wood construction and come in size gradations of 2 feet. Some manufacturers, notably several British firms, have a system of glass installation that requires no glazing, and replacement is extremely easy. At least one firm specializing in economical home greenhouses has recently offered for sale several balcony models as small as 3′3″ by 2′3″ by 5′ high. Some of these have a special glazing that will resist high wind conditions.

Another way of having a greenhouse on your balcony is to use a series of plastic panels on spring-mounted framework, a type of construction that eliminates the problems involved in installing a permanent structure. Panels and framework would be in place from October to May only, so that the balcony could revert to an outdoor garden during the summer.

By converting all or part of your balcony into a greenhouse you are really adding another room to your apartment. The added maintenance costs are minimal, and, provided the capital cost can be amortized over several years, a greenhouse that provides both food and flowers could well prove to be an advantageous as well as a satisfying undertaking.

Annuals:
Flowers and Vines

Your choice of plants – annuals, perennials, or trees and shrubs – could depend on which method of balcony gardening you prefer: containers or a floor garden (see Chapter 3). Alternatively, if you have in mind some favourite flowers that you are determined to grow, your method of gardening could depend on the size and type of those flowers. But from whichever direction you approach your balcony garden, you will probably want to include in it at least a few colourful annuals so that you are sure of enjoying a continuous display of buds and bloom throughout the summer months.

When you are planning a balcony garden, try to be at home for a day or two in each of the late spring and summer months to watch for how long and when the sun strikes which parts of your balcony. You will have greater success with your garden if your choice of plants is guided by the amount of sun or light they prefer.

Flowers in the Sun

If your balcony, or part of it, receives an average of three hours of sunshine every day, you will be able to grow any of the annuals that need sun.

Petunias are certainly the most popular of all annuals, and have been so for the past ten years, judging by their sales. Thousands of varieties are available, and to simplify our discussion these may be classified into two main groups: multifloras, which bear large quantities of 2- to 3-inch flowers on plants 10 to 15 inches tall, and grandifloras, which bear slightly fewer but larger blooms (3¾ to 4 inches in diameter) on plants 11 to 15 inches high. Both groups include double-flowering petunias, some with large flowers, other with small, and the petunias of greatest importance in container gardening – the cascade varieties.

Most cascade petunias are really grandifloras, but because of their importance to balcony gardening I am treating them as a special group so that they will be given the attention they deserve. Cascades are the best of the petunias not only for hanging baskets but for window boxes and floor-level containers. They are available in a wide range of colours including pink, coral, red, and dark blue, as well as in white. When you are planting cascade petunias, put them towards the outside of the container so that their trailing branches may easily reach over the edge. The variety 'Sugar Daddy', though not a cascade, is also very suitable for containers, because it tends to grow in the same trailing manner as the cascades. This variety has mauve ruffled blooms on which the thin deep-purple veins clearly stand out.

Cascade petunias are the most popular of the petunias for container planting because of their natural pendulous habit. In late August, however reluctant you feel about removing buds and flowers, try pruning all the stems back to 7 or 8 inches and applying liquid fertilizer (15-30-15) to encourage a new crop of autumn bloom.

Other varieties of grandiflora worth watching for at your corner market or garden supply store are 'Calypso', 'Appleblossom', 'Red Magic', and also 'Sky Magic' – a delightful light blue with a magnificent strong scent at night. In the multiflora group watch for varieties named 'Red Devil', 'White Joy', and the older but reliable 'Coral Satin', still one of the best. Two double-flowering varieties to bring home, if you see them, are 'Valentine' (light red, of course) and 'Orchid Bouquet', which has 3½-inch, darker-veined, pale mauve flowers on plants 12 inches tall.

While petunias will provide a show of continuous colour lasting four months, with little effort on your part, it is advisable to water them once a month with a liquid fertilizer high in phosphate, to encourage flowers and a strong root system. Use a formula with a high middle number, perhaps 15-30-15, which indicates that the mixture contains 30 per cent phosphate. In common with most plants, petunias like good drainage, and they prefer full sun.

The actual amount of light at railing height on the edge of a balcony facing north or east is almost the same as at ground level in a garden that is shaded for certain periods each day by trees and buildings. Therefore, even if your balcony faces east or north, do not rule out sun-loving plants such as petunias. Most of them will grow well, though you will probably discover that some varieties do much better than others. In fact a few varieties of petunia, such as 'Chiffon Cascade' and 'Pink Lace', which are delicate in colour, grow much better in semi-shade than they do in full sun, where their colours bleach. If your balcony is shaded for most of the day, perhaps because other buildings are so close, you might study the annuals that are particularly tolerant of shade; some of these are discussed later in this chapter. But try a number of the sun-loving plants first, before you entirely discard the idea of growing them; their performance may surprise you.

Second in popularity of the sun-loving annuals are the marigolds, another diverse group of plants extremely well suited to container planting. Only recently have marigolds shown an increase in popularity, mainly because an almost scentless quality has been successfully bred into some of the new hybrid varieties. There is now much less of the objectionable but unmistakable marigold odour in many of the varieties, particularly the beautiful new ones.

Marigolds can still be divided into two groups, as they have been for many years: the tall African types, which easily reach 30 to 36 inches in height, and the dwarf French hybrids. However, new varieties have been developed that exhibit the more desirable qualities of both types – the large flowers of the African on small plants not much taller than the French hybrids. Two recent introductions are 'Moonshot' and 'Apollo', both 14 inches high, which begin to bloom when they are only 10 inches tall. The flowers of 'Moonshot' are brilliant yellow, those of 'Apollo' deep orange; the flowers of both varieties are semi-double and about 3 inches in diameter.

Two varieties similar to 'Moonshot' and 'Apollo' that are worth trying along the centre of your railing boxes are 'Spun Gold' and 'Spun Yellow'. These plants grow about 12 inches high and bear double flowers almost 3 inches in diameter. Others which have impressed me in various trials are 'King Tut', 10 inches high, whose bright-yellow centres contrast with rich mahogany outer petals, and the semi-double 'Spanish Brocade', offering red and yellow-gold 2-inch blooms on plants 12 inches high. If you prefer the taller African types – perhaps to use in the centre of a large floor-level container – then look for the red-and-gold 'Climax' varieties. Seven 'Climax Yellow' marigolds planted in the centre of a container 30 inches in diameter, surrounded by at least a dozen 'Sugar Daddy' petunias and edged with another dozen cascading red petunias – or these intermixed with trailing German ivy (*Senecio mikanioides*) – should make a simple yet most effective planting for the entire growing season.

Just by using marigolds, petunias, and ivy you will be able to dream up many other striking colour combinations – but don't stop there: look also at the wide range of other plants available. Let us consider briefly some of the other popular annual flowers, as well as some that are certainly as beautiful, though not as well known.

Sweet alyssum, most commonly used as a border plant by ground-level gardeners, is also suited to container planting. But the plant, though it does not grow more than about 4 inches tall, will spread rapidly and should be considered as an edging only for larger containers. Another dwarf plant, one of the best for retaining its bright colours in the sun, is portulaca. The recently introduced double-flowering varieties provide a rainbow of colour, the individual flowers resembling little roses and often exceeding 2 inches in diameter. All this just 5 inches from the surface of the soil! Try one railing box with a row of celosia 'Fairy Fountains Mixed' down the centre and mixed portulaca around the edges.

Celosia resembles vivid red, orange, and yellow brushes or brooms emerging from bright-green foliage and growing, on average, 12 inches in height. In addition to portulaca, a second companion for celosia is ageratum, and you may be able to obtain the especially pretty hybrid variety 'Hybrid Blue Mink', growing 6 inches tall, which has clusters of tiny powder-blue flowers. This variety, or a similar one if you are unable to find 'Blue Mink', will contrast well with 'Fairy Fountains Mixed' celosia.

If you have toured any of the public or private greenhouses at about Easter time, you may have marvelled at the unusual beauty of the calceolarias, with their pouch-like flower parts often exceeding 1½ inches across. A newer variety of this popular greenhouse plant performs well in balcony containers: *Calceolaria* 'Dwarf Sunshine' grows to a height of 12 inches, and is covered with tiny lemon-yellow flowers in the characteristic pouch-like shape all summer long. Try half a dozen of these in a window box or hanging basket edged with lobelia. The lobelia best suited to container planting is *Lobelia pendula* 'Sapphire', which has a somewhat drooping habit, so that it will hang over the edge of the container. Its many tiny deep-blue flowers each have a white 'eye'. Bear in mind that because lobelia does not recover well

The newest members of the snapdragon family are the open-faced varieties, called 'butterfly snaps'. Like the older form of snapdragon, the new ones will bloom continuously if you keep cutting off the flowers once they are past their best.

Calceolarias (sometimes called 'pocketbook flowers' from the pouch-like formation of the bloom) are unusual and colourful annual plants.

OPEN FACED SNAPDRAGON

CALCEOLARIAS

once it has been allowed to dry out, the soil should be kept slightly moist at all times.

If you like scarlet to brighten your scene throughout the summer, but you want a change from petunias, consider salvia. The varieties 'Jet Fire' and 'St. John's Fire' are among the best and they grow only to a maximum height of 13 inches. If you are already a salvia enthusiast, you may want to try 'Purple Flame', whose flowers live up to the name. A group of 'Purple Flame' in bloom, surrounded by a circle of 'St. John's Fire', contrast with each other dramatically; try one container in which the two are mixed together and you will hear plenty of comments from your balcony visitors.

Remember when snapdragons were called that because their flowers had tubular throats and snapping jaws? That description no longer fits all the modern snapdragons, for a new form that has open-faced flowers resembling those of the azalea was introduced in the early 1970s. And now, in addition to this new azalea-flowered type, there are semi-dwarf forms with the same beautifully shaped flower. The 'Sweetheart' variety is 12 inches high, with colours ranging from red to yellow and white. If you like snapdragons, try to obtain some of these, especially if the wind tends to sweep across your balcony, for the 'Sweetheart' plants branch from the base and withstand wind better than most of the other varieties. But if it's the typical snapdragon with the snapping jaws you want, the semi-dwarfs are probably the most convenient size for containers – look for 'Carioca Outdoor Finest Mixed', which grow to a height of 20 inches.

Among the best of the old standby annuals are the zinnias, which I have not yet mentioned. Seed hybridizers have done a good deal of work on zinnias, as on the flowers mentioned earlier in this chapter, resulting in the development of several new varieties that are particularly suited to container growing. Have a look especially for zinnias of the Peter Pan series, which produce flowers 3 inches wide or more, in varying colours, on plants 12 inches tall. When you buy Peter Pan zinnias in early spring, the plants may well not be in bloom, but the flowers will appear by early July and are worth waiting for. Plant a container or a railing box with Peter Pan and edge it with sweet alyssum.

Verbena venosa 'Lilacena' is an old annual flower that is currently attracting renewed attention. The somewhat creeping plants, 8 inches high, support many lilac-blue flower clusters from late June until frost. This variety is best massed in a fairly large container that has three taller red flowers in the centre; for the centre try salvia 'Jet Fire', for instance, whose red blooms will grow tall enough to show above the verbena. There are other verbenas as well, and for an effective show of mixed colour you can hardly beat the 'Rainbow Mixture'. Use verbenas instead of petunias: they will be a change from the petunias, will lend a slightly different character to your container plantings, but will give an effect just as cheerfully colourful.

Geraniums are very popular as container plants. Though they are not annuals, but perennials, they are usually treated as annuals if they are to be grown on balconies. Containers holding an arrangement of traditional plants, still seen in many garden centres, include a dracaena (*Dracaena indivisa*) in the centre with its sword-like leaves pointing to the sky, surrounded by red geraniums, and usually some German ivy trailing over the edge. Obviously, there is little to say against this traditional planting except that dracaenas and geraniums are among the most expensive plants that could be chosen for containers. Their cost is high simply because more time is involved in growing them than other species; dracaenas, for example, take nearly two years to reach salable size.

Most geraniums are grown from cuttings of older plants, but if you would like to try a new and vigorous geranium, look for the new type grown from seed – 'Sprinter', for example, whose flowers are a brilliant red. Though usually recommended only for sunny locations, geraniums will also thrive on shaded east- and north-facing balconies.

There are three other annuals, not so well known as those I have discussed so far, but worth hunting for. *Thunbergia alata*, the annual

The annual black-eyed Susan, with its orange-yellow flowers and black 'eye', provides an ideal edging for hanging baskets.

black-eyed Susan, is an ideal vine-like plant for containers or hanging baskets. For most of the growing season the green foliage is covered with hundreds of small orange-to-yellow flowers, each with a black centre. A variety that has larger flowers, 'Gibsoni', is also available. As with lobelia, do not allow the soil in which the black-eyed Susans are growing to dry out entirely; if you do, the plants will cease blooming. Nasturtiums are a reliable annual not demanding a rich soil; in fact they prefer no added fertilizer once they have been planted in their container. Gomphrena, also called globe amaranth, is a dwarf plant whose flowers closely resemble those of large, fully-grown red clover. Gomphrena can easily be dried by being hung upside-down in the dark for three or four days in dry heat, and once dried the flowers are suitable for use in winter bouquets.

You may wish to grow the miniature double button English daisy (*Bellis perennis* 'Miniature Double Button'), which is a perennial normally used as an annual. If you buy the plants they will be expensive, since they must be started from seed at least six months earlier than annuals. The tiny double flowers, however, will be more than sufficient reward for your perseverence in seeking out the plant – or in growing it yourself from seed.

Such a large number of annuals suitable for balcony containers are available that I have only been able to suggest a representative selection. Many other varieties of the annuals discussed here could be successfully grown by the balcony gardener, so could numerous other species (*Gazania, Nicotiana, Santolina*, for example) which I have not even mentioned. Each one has its own particularly desirable attribute, and each one merits the balcony gardener's consideration. *Nicotiana*, for example, is noted for its strong, heavy fragrance in the evening; the common, tall-growing, white variety is the most fragrant, though its flowers remain closed most of the day.

Regardless of which annual flowers you choose for your containers, if you want a good display of colour for at least three-and-a-half months, rather than just for the last two weeks of August and in early September when the plants reach maturity, you should plant the young plants closer together than is recommended for ground-level gardening. Many books on container planting recommend wide spacing for plants in containers – as few as three or four cascade petunias in a 9- or 10-inch hanging basket. In common with other experienced container gardeners in this northern climate, I recommend these two rules of thumb: for round containers, approximately one plant for each inch in diameter of the container; for square or rectangular containers, one plant for every 18 square inches of soil surface – for these containers simply multiply the inside length by the width, then divide by 18 to obtain the approximate number of plants you will need. Although these recommended spacings may seem to crowd the plants, the overall effect of the plantings will be beautiful for the maximum length of time.

Vines

Annual vines should not be disregarded for balconies: they are ideal for creating screens to give privacy, and on a warm evening can lend a tropical atmosphere even to the most urban balcony. Morning glory (*Ipomoea purpurea*) and moonflower (*Calonyction aculeatum*), two vines in the morning glory family, will grow at least 12 feet high. Both need the support of a trellis or strings, but it is not necessary to build a heavy permanent structure for them. These vines grow best if they are started from seed where they are to grow.

One of the taller-growing annuals, the castor oil bean (*Ricinus*) can be grouped with the vines since it is often planted to perform the same function. There are two types of castor oil bean: *Ricinus sanguineus*, which has reddish leaves on black stems and grows to 8 feet in height by mid-August, and *Ricinus zanzibariensis*, which has green

Castor oil bean plants grow to their full height in one season. Your neighbours will think you have chosen to live in the tropics, and may also decide to try some green seclusion. This plant, 2 feet high, has been growing outdoors for only a month.

leaves and grows to 15 feet. Castor oil bean plants are available from nurseries or they may be started indoors from seed. But beware – the seeds are poisonous. If you have children around, you should probably forget about starting your castor oil beans from seed and buy plants instead.

One of the most interesting annual vines grows to only about 50 inches tall – the double-flowering blue morning glory. Though the plants also have some single flowers, double violet-blue blooms edged in white predominate and remain open most of the day.

If your balcony is open on several sides, and you wish to use annual vines to close it in partially, you may need a wider selection of vines than those I have suggested so far. Try the cup-and-saucer vine or cathedral bells (*Cobaea scandens*), which attains a height of 20 feet or more; other annual climbers you might consider are four-o'clocks, kudzu (*Pueraria thunbergia*), nasturtiums, and scarlet runner beans. These particular climbers are difficult to obtain as started plants, and you should therefore start them yourself from seed indoors about the second week of May as briefly described later in this chapter, or directly outdoors after May 24, depending on your climate.

Colour for Shaded Balconies

Should your balcony be very shaded, you will want to be familiar with the names of some of the plants you may expect to find at your local plant dealer's that will thrive in the shade. One of the most popular, impatiens, is now available in several different series of dwarf varieties. The common name of impatiens is, oddly enough, patience plant; appropriate in that the varieties are certainly very patient with shady conditions. In fact, one of the newer dwarf forms, the Elfin series which grows to a height of only 6 inches, does not thrive in the sun. Almost every plant dealer – whether a garden centre or the local fruit and vegetable store – has impatiens, usually in an array of colours from white to pink, salmon, fuchsia, orange, red, scarlet, orchid, and even purple. If you decide to plant this annual, look for a sales outlet that carries a wide selection of plants, so that you have a choice of flower colours.

By choosing a couple of boxes of impatiens – one box of dwarf plants, perhaps 'Elfin Rose', and another of a taller variety, possibly 'Holistic' in a scarlet or purple range – you will be able to plant a container on your shady balcony that will give you a continuous bouquet of colour from June until frost. If the container is 30 inches or more in diameter, you might also consider planting a border of sweet alyssum, which will also tolerate some shade, particularly on north- and east-facing balconies at high levels. Remember that geraniums (including the varieties with multi-coloured leaves) will grow in shade, and you should not hesitate to plant some even if your balcony is continuously shaded.

Other plants, too, will thrive on a shady balcony and provide colour throughout the season. Try some of the many hybrid fibrous begonias. These green- and red-leaved little plants, some with double flowers, are available all year round and may be grown indoors as well as out. Look for white, pink, or red flowers, and keep in mind that in full shade the green-leaved varieties fare better than the bronze- or red-leaved kinds.

You may already be familiar with tuberous begonias: perhaps you have watched or helped your gardening friends encourage those dry, dead-looking tubers to produce tall plants. Tuberous begonias are available as potted and staked plants in early June, but if you start planning early enough, you will save a great deal of money by buying the tubers in early March and starting them off yourself.

Plant the begonia tubers concave side up in shallow flats, pans, or pots, no more than half an inch below the surface. The best mixture in which to start them is leaf mould, which may be difficult to obtain. As an alternative, use 50 per cent each of peat moss and perlite, both available from garden supply outlets, larger hardware stores, and major department stores. Water the tubers, but bear in mind that while they like to be kept moist they may rot if kept too wet. When the plants reach a height of 2½ to 3 inches, transplant them into individual 5-inch pots – the bottom sections of 2-quart milk cartons are adequate provided you punch drainage holes in them. Prepare a potting mixture of a third each of peat moss, sharp sand, and perlite. Ideally, leaf mould or similar organic compost should be substituted for the perlite, if it is available.

When all danger of frost has passed and you plant the begonias out on your balcony, the following two hints may be useful. First, the flowers are always borne facing the same direction in which the leaves point; therefore, if your containers are fixed in place or if you do not intend to move them once they have been filled, be certain to plant the begonias with the leaves pointing so that you will be able to see the full beauty of the flowers. Second, as the flowers develop, you will

Start your begonia tubers in March. Plant the tubers with their tops uppermost – bearing in mind that the top is the concave side of the tuber, and that it usually has one or two pink shoots (not roots) showing.

When the foliage reaches 2½ to 3 inches in height, transplant the tubers into 5-inch flowerpots. Let the tubers grow there until you move them to their summer positions on the balcony, when there is no more likelihood of frost. Before you leave them outside for the whole summer, on warm spring days set the pots outside to accustom the plants to the varying temperatures and winds, bringing them in again if frost is expected. As the plants grow taller, small stakes may be needed to support their large heavy flower stems.

see that there are two distinct kinds. Though on each plant all the flowers will be the same colour, some will be large, full, and have frilly petals, others will appear smaller and not perfectly circular. The smaller ones are the male flowers, which are not nearly as pretty as the female flowers. If you remove the male flowers before they develop, more strength will go into the production of the beautiful female flowers. Be careful, though, that you remove only the male flowers; let them all grow to a size sufficient for you to see what you are doing.

One of the most popular modern types of begonia, the Rieger, originated in Europe. Though these begonias are being made popular by flower growers in North America as the ideal house plant, their use out-of-doors in balcony containers during the summer is still to be recognized here. Rieger begonias are sold as small (young) and large flowering plants during most seasons of the year. If your balcony is in shade or semi-shade for much of the day, try one or two: you will soon become enthusiastic about them.

One final plant for shade is coleus, which comes in numerous varieties all grown for their beautifully coloured leaves. The flowers are insignificant and you would be well advised to pinch them out before they develop. The only kinds of coleus not worth planting in full shade are those producing yellow leaves; without full sun, this foliage will just be green. All the other varieties will grow well in shade. Look especially for a newly developed series known as Carefree coleus; plants in this series have unusually ruffled leaves and interesting colour variations.

There is a disappointingly small choice of plants for hanging baskets that must be placed in shade, though there is enough variety to warrant your filling a basket or two to give colour on your shady balcony. Specialized varieties of tuberous begonia, called 'Pendula', are available in various colours. Lobelia is another annual that will perform well in shade: it will produce a multitude of tiny light- or dark-blue flowers on trailing stems over the side of your hanging baskets. 'Blue Cascade' has light-blue flowers and contrasts well with the darker blue 'Sapphire', which has a white 'eye'. If you are looking for a leafy trailing plant, you will find it difficult to surpass spider plant (*Chlorophytum elatum* 'Variegatum'), which has white-and-green striped grass-like leaves. At the ends of its long flower stems new plants are produced; these may be cut off and potted for use indoors all winter. Also suited to hanging baskets is the climber Bougainvillea, which is usually obtainable only from indoor plant suppliers. Dwarf impatiens, too, will provide colour lasting throughout the season.

Transplanting Your Annuals

Annual flowers, such as the ones I have just described, are sold through a variety of outlets and are packaged in at least two quite different ways. By far the oldest method, flats (holding twenty-four or more plants) and small boxes (six to eight plants) in which plants of a single variety are growing in a common soil area, is in declining use

Increasingly popular with those who like to grow annual plants are the small plastic packs, each plant growing in its own individual compartment of soil. When you are planting from these, be sure to remove the plant from its compartment and break up the soil slightly, so that the roots will be encouraged to spread out into the soil of the container.

today. When you are transplanting from these boxes, simply pull a fistful of soil surrounding each plant away from the remainder, and plant it so that the soil around the new plant is even with that in your container or floor garden. In the new method of packaging (also used for tomato plants, for example), individual tiny packets of soil in a plastic container are used for each plant. When transplanting these, it is advisable to break up the soil and roots slightly before planting, in order to encourage the plants to send out new roots into the soil. If your new plants have been grown in thin pressed peat (moss) pots, be sure the upper rims of the pots are beneath the soil level in your containers, and break up the pot and small root ball slightly before transplanting. Finally, regardless of the origin of your plants and how they were packaged, an application of a transplanter fertilizer (10-45-15) will speed up their recovery after you have arranged them in their permanent positions.

Starting Annuals Yourself

Though it is easy to pick up the annual flowers you need in boxes at the corner market or local garden centre, there is much to be said for growing some or all of the plants from seed yourself. Caught in today's inflationary spiral, many apartment gardeners find that once they have invested in the necessary equipment, they do save money growing their own plants. The other major point in favour of starting from seed is that many more varieties are available from seed houses in January and February than are on sale as plants even in the best-stocked garden centre in May and early June.

To start seeds, some basic equipment is needed: this is readily available and can be fitted into a relatively small space. Although some varieties may be started off in a sunny window, the light is often not strong enough during winter and early spring to ensure success with every type of seed, and the ideal method is to start the seeds under a 24- or 48-inch fluorescent fixture. The most satisfactory units are those which provide for one or two small incandescent (regular) light bulbs to be inserted between two fluorescent tubes. If you wish to set up a unit extremely economically, obtain a used fixture from a building that is being torn down or renovated. A socket or two for incandescent bulbs may easily be added, and the repainted unit set on a kitchen shelf or window sill as a decorative feature.

There are at least half a dozen media suitable for starting seeds. These include a mixture of peat moss and perlite; a combination of milled sphagnum moss and sand; sterilized soil, and so on. A number of specially prepared mixtures for starting seeds are also available. Any of these may be used, and provided your container is clean, you should have little difficulty in starting your seeds. Large seeds (such as

Vegetable and flower seeds may be started under fluorescent lights. For best results, the lights should be only a few inches above the seedlings, a distance that can be maintained by lowering the seedlings as they grow taller or by raising the height of the lights.

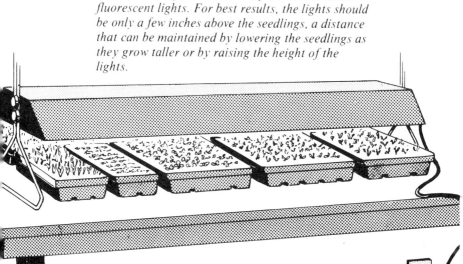

marigolds and zinnias) should be covered with the starting medium to no more than twice their thickness, while small seeds (such as petunias) need only be slightly pressed into the medium. Most seeds, with the exception of impatiens, will germinate in darkness, and do so faster if the container is covered with a piece of thin plastic (a dry cleaner's protective bag, for example), but remove the plastic as soon as the seeds show signs of germinating.

If you are starting seeds under fluorescent lights, lower the lights or raise the container holding the seeds so that the lights are only a few inches from the seedlings. While germinating, seedlings like to have a warm starting medium (70°F, 21°C), but they develop better if the air temperature itself is lower (60°F, 16°C), particularly at night (55°F, 13°C). This combination is often difficult to achieve within the confines of a small apartment, and if a compromise must be made, it is better to choose good light and a cool air temperature. By using your ingenuity, you may be able to supply some heat from below for the starting medium on a cool window sill by putting your seed container on top of a radio, for example.

The mistake perhaps most often made by amateurs is to start the seeds too early. Many young seedlings are wasted because they grow too tall, then become limp and die, having been started 4 to 6 weeks before it was necessary. Only a few varieties, such as petunias, browallia, and ageratum, need be started early – on or about March 1. Lobelia and nicotine should be started in the middle of March. None of the other annuals mentioned in this section need be started until April 1, and many, such as castor oil bean and marigolds, may be started after April 15 – even as late as May 1. Fluorescent lights should remain on for approximately sixteen hours a day; however, if the seedlings start to become leggy, you should slow down their rate of growth by reducing the number of hours of light to about twelve. Most seed catalogues provide detailed information about starting seeds.

It is not necessary to start all your annuals from seed indoors: many annual seeds can be sown outdoors directly where they are to grow. Examples are ageratum and snapdragons about May 1; coleus, marigolds, moonflowers, morning glory, sweet alyssum, and zinnias from about May 24 to June 1.

Annual plants started indoors need to be 'hardened off' before being taken outdoors permanently for the summer. This acclimatization is best done by first introducing the seedlings to the out-of-doors on a calm warm day for a couple of hours. Be sure you do not place them in the direct sun. After this initial exposure, the length of time may be gradually lengthened until the plants are left outside, though you might cover them with newspaper when an unusually cold night is expected. The young plants should then be transplanted into the appropriate containers, baskets, and boxes no earlier than May 24.

Taking Cuttings

Annuals, in addition to being started from seed, may also be propagated from cuttings. Almost all the annuals discussed in this chapter may easily be started from stem cuttings (without flowers) taken from plants of the same variety. For reasons unknown, even experienced gardeners who efficiently and successfully propagate indoor plants as well as some of the outdoor hardy shrubs and trees from cuttings do not realize that annual flowers may easily be reproduced in this way. However, you do need to have the plants from which to take the cuttings available to you.

Cuttings of some plants (impatiens and geraniums, for instance) may be taken from the plant growing outdoors in September, just before the first frost. To help the rooting process, dip the cut end of

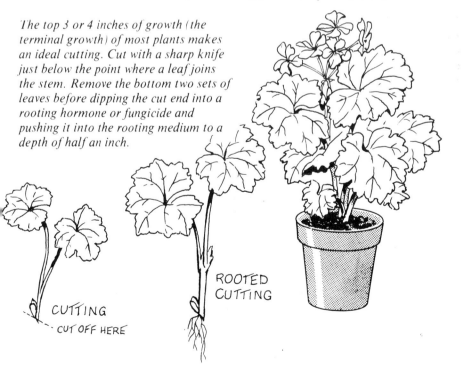

The top 3 or 4 inches of growth (the terminal growth) of most plants makes an ideal cutting. Cut with a sharp knife just below the point where a leaf joins the stem. Remove the bottom two sets of leaves before dipping the cut end into a rooting hormone or fungicide and pushing it into the rooting medium to a depth of half an inch.

ROOTED CUTTING

CUTTING

CUT OFF HERE

the cutting into a rooting hormone, usually available only at garden supply and major department stores, or plant fungicide such as captan 50 W (50 per cent wettable powder) to prevent rotting and disease. Root the cuttings by inserting them in a rooting medium such as perlite, vermiculite, or clean sharp sand, and covering them with plastic. In ten days to three weeks' time (according to the species of plant) there should be signs of root formation: the cutting will feel firm when you tug slightly at the stem. When a strong root system has formed, the new plants should be potted and grown on window sills or under fluorescent lights. Plants rooted in this way during the autumn will provide excellent stock plants from which to take further cuttings the following March or April (depending on the rate of growth) for planting outoors in your containers in the summer.

Some annuals do not grow well indoors during the winter because there is insufficient light for them and the temperature is too high – among these are marigolds, zinnias, and petunias. If you buy just one box each of your favourite varieties as early as possible in the spring – even before planting-out time – you may multiply the number of plants by taking 2½-inch cuttings and rooting them in the way I have described in this section.

Colour If You Move In During the Summer

How can you manage to grow a balcony garden if you happen to move into an apartment in late June or in July? By this time, most plant dealers have sold their supply of boxed annuals, and it may be impossible for you to find any healthy-looking plants to liven up your empty balcony. Before you decide to take cuttings from plants grown by your friends on their balconies or in their ground-level gardens, find out whether there are any annuals available from the larger garden centres. If the answer is no, propagate your own by taking 2½- to 3-inch cuttings, removing any flowers and the bottom leaves, and rooting them as described in the previous section.

Should you move into an apartment with an unplanted balcony after August 1, forget about annual flowers. Instead, buy potted or balled and burlapped chrysanthemums from a large nursery or garden centre. A wide choice of flower types, on plants of varying heights, is available, and they will begin to bloom in mid-September. Look especially for the series called Masterpiece, consisting of fourteen or more different varieties.

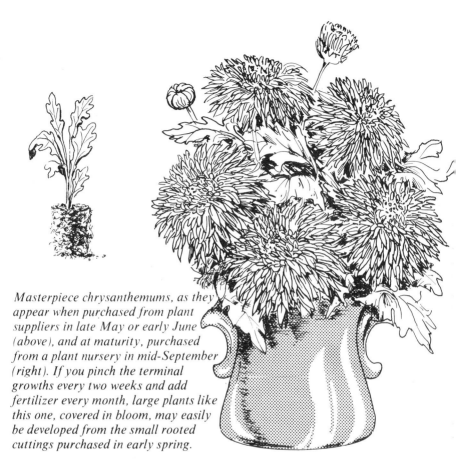

Masterpiece chrysanthemums, as they appear when purchased from plant suppliers in late May or early June (above), and at maturity, purchased from a plant nursery in mid-September (right). If you pinch the terminal growths every two weeks and add fertilizer every month, large plants like this one, covered in bloom, may easily be developed from the small rooted cuttings purchased in early spring.

Balcony gardeners who particularly want a striking display of colour in the autumn should reserve at least one container for this type of chrysanthemum. Bought in the early spring as small rooted cuttings either packaged or in small pots, they are economical and require little care through the summer as they develop into beautiful large plants for the fall display. From the time they are planted until mid-July, all the new growth shoots on each plant should be pinched out every two weeks to make the plants bushy. A liquid fertilizer may be added each month, and the plants kept watered as needed. The containers in which you plant the chrysanthemums should be 30 inches in diameter, and if you have short and tall varieties the taller ones should be in the centre surrounded by lower-growing plants of a contrasting colour.

Care of Annuals Through the Summer

Although you must water your balcony annuals regularly, annual flowers in containers make few other demands of their gardener. A liquid fertilizer with a formula such as 15-30-15 applied once a month, or even every third week, will improve them – though nasturtiums are an exception, for they need little fertilizer.

The intervals between watering may be lengthened by covering the soil in the pot with a mulch, by inserting insulation material such as styrofoam or foam rubber between the soil and the side of the container, and by choosing containers light in colour that reflect rather than absorb the sun's rays.

Most annual plants will benefit from being cut back sometime in early or mid-August. If your petunias, sweet alyssum, snapdragons, lobelia, ageratum, or other annuals begin to look leggy and unattractive, cut half to two-thirds off each growing stem. For a week, or even less, the plants will look worse, but soon new growth will appear and the containers will be better than ever with much new bloom. This cutting back is particularly effective if it is followed immediately by an application of liquid fertilizer.

Balcony Vegetables, Herbs, and Fruits

Vegetable growing in back gardens began to decline in North America during the 1960s, but less than ten years later, with the sharp rises in the cost of food – including fresh vegetables – this decline was halted, to be replaced by a new upswing in popularity. The demand for vegetable seeds in the 1974 spring season was so great that at least one seedhouse had to delay filling orders while it waited for new supplies.

Many apartment dwellers are unaware that it is possible for them to grow vegetables on their balconies all summer and herbs on their kitchen or living-room window sills all year round; in other words, apartment dwellers can now join the increasing number of vegetable growers. The selection of vegetables that will thrive on a balcony is almost as wide as for gardens at ground level, and the ones I suggest in this chapter for container growing are only those that adapt most easily to restricted growth in containers. Many other vegetables, in addition to the ones discussed here, can be successfully grown on balconies. But in choosing to grow vegetables or fruits on your balcony, you should be prepared to give a little extra effort above and beyond planting the plants and harvesting the crop. The work is not arduous, but 'little and often' might well be the key phrase to your success. To feel like a true grower of plants, start the seeds yourself; it is often rather difficult, for example, to obtain varieties of tomato plants suitable for balconies from plant sellers – you stand a better chance of succeeding as a vegetable gardener if you start from seed.

Tomatoes

The most popular vegetable for balcony growing is not a vegetable at all, but a fruit – the tomato. Though many apartment gardeners have grown tomatoes successfully, many have been less fortunate – perhaps because they tried inappropriate varieties or gave their plants too little care by forgetting to water them or failing to spray them. They may even have attempted to grow them on a completely shaded balcony, not knowing that the few fruit produced by a tomato plant receiving no sun will taste unpleasantly acid when ripe.

In February, if you have not received a seed catalogue, write and obtain at least one (see Sources, p. 118). Read the information about how to grow vegetables from seed given both generally and for the specific varieties. You will find, for instance, that a variety of tomato known as 'Stakeless' is ideal for containers because it grows to a height of only 20 inches and has abundant foliage to protect the fruit from sun scald. Maturing in about ten weeks, which means that you will be able to pick the first tomatoes by that time, 'Stakeless' is suitable for areas such as southern Ontario where long growing seasons of eighteen weeks are normal. For more northerly areas, earlier maturing varieties such as 'Early Girl' and 'Tiny Tim' are recommended. These mature in only forty-five days, so from plants put out in containers around May 24 (not earlier) you may expect your first tomatoes by the middle of July. In colder regions where plants cannot safely be put out permanently until mid-June, the first fruit would be expected towards the end of July.

If you are starting tomatoes from seed, be sure not to start them too early: April 1 is about right in most areas – in cold regions even April 15 is early enough. When the seedlings have developed their first set of true leaves, they should be transplanted to small individual pots. Tomatoes, like annual flowers, are best grown in cool temperatures (60 °F, 16 °C) and prefer an almost dry soil to a moist one. On warm days, they should be moved outside to acclimatize them and slow their growth.

Be sure to choose sufficiently large containers for your tomatoes: 10 inches deep with an inside top diameter of 12 inches is best, but for strong root development plant only one of all except the miniature varieties in a pot this size. Use fresh soil, or soil from previous plantings rejuvenated with one-third fresh soil mix. I recommend a commercial soil mix increased by a third with sharp clean sand or perlite.

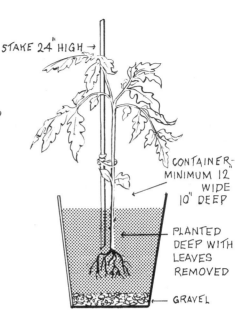

STAKE 24" HIGH →

CONTAINER-
MINIMUM 12"
WIDE
10" DEEP

PLANTED
DEEP WITH
LEAVES
REMOVED

GRAVEL

When you plant your tomato plants, remember that they will greatly increase in size, and though the young plants may look ridiculous at first in a container 12 inches in diameter, you will find that they soon require all the growing space you have given them.

When planting tomato plants in your containers, be sure that there is no further danger of frost. Planting them out early will not produce an earlier crop, for tomato plants originated in a hot climate and they go into a state of suspended growth if the temperature falls below 40°F (4°C). It is better to bring the plants indoors on cool nights than to plant them permanently in your containers too early. In planting, remove all but the top two sets of leaves and plunge the plants into holes deep enough for the largest set of leaves to be just at soil level. This technique will allow the plant to send out additional roots from the stem into the soil. Though the variety you chose may be 'Stakeless', you should nevertheless push a stake into the container beside each plant to support it during high winds and to prevent heavy fruit from weighing it down to breaking point. As the plant grows, it should be tied to the stake every 4 or 5 inches, preferably with inch-wide strips of cloth, to prevent damage to its stem.

Liquid fertilizer (a formula such as 15-30-15) should be added once every three weeks. Mixed according to directions, it may be poured right over the foliage and the excess allowed to drip down onto the soil in the container. As an alternative, you might use the fertilizer now available that lasts throughout the season (see p.13).

Since different varieties of many vegetables have different maturing

7½"

FULL GROWTH

If each 'Tiny Tim' tomato plant is to be grown in a separate container, a pot only about 6 inches in diameter will give the plant sufficient space to grow.

times (days needed from seeding to first harvest), be certain to consult your seed catalogue for this information before you order.

Earlier in this discussion of tomato plants, I mentioned the variety 'Tiny Tim'. The best of the cherry tomatoes, it is ideally suited to container growing since it seldom exceeds 10 inches in height and the plants bear an abundance of the tiny tomatoes. Three plants of this early maturing variety may be planted in a pot with an inside diameter of 12 inches, and little or no staking will be required. If you have a fluorescent light fixture in your apartment no more than 30 inches away from a surface on which plant pots can be set, you will find it possible to grow 'Tiny Tim' plants throughout the autumn, winter, and spring seasons.

Regardless of which variety of tomato plant you grow, it will do better if you regularly remove the sucker growths that develop in the axils of any two major stems. These should be pinched out as they appear. To promote fleshier and less seedy fruit, and to ensure fruit in the absence of bees (especially indoors), spray each new set of yellow flowers with a blossom-set spray, following carefully the directions on the can. This treatment will be a great help to the development of your crop.

Growing Other Vegetables

The best soil for growing all varieties of vegetables is the same as I have described for tomatoes (p. 58). As for the best type of container

– except for tomatoes, cucumbers, eggplants, and other plants that grow to a very large size, all vegetables may be successfully grown even in a window box or railing box. The larger-growing vegetables should be grown in the same type of containers suggested for tomatoes. Like tomatoes, most vegetables demand full sun; however, if yours is a bright east- or north-facing balcony, you should try some of the kinds discussed in the remainder of the chapter in the lightest place on your balcony.

Having detailed the easy steps to growing tomatoes on your balcony, I now want to suggest a number of other vegetables that you will find just as easy to grow – though rather less common in balcony gardens.

Better Salads

Of the other basic salad ingredients in addition to tomatoes, lettuce is one that you can easily grow in containers, and, once you have grown your own, you will dislike having to return to bought heads again in the fall. The reason for the flavourless quality of the lettuce sold in the stores is that these varieties have been especially developed to suit a set of standards dictated by the growers and shippers of lettuce as well as by those who market it. These standards have led to a number of excellent varieties of lettuce able to withstand long periods of time from picking to purchase, but flavour has been almost forgotten. Judging by the taste, one might think there was almost as much cellulose in the lettuce itself as in its cellophane wrapping. So for flavour in lettuce try 'Butterking' or 'Buttercrunch' seeded directly into your outdoor containers as soon after April 15 as the soil is workable. This gourmet lettuce makes a salad all by itself. Just cut the plant off at soil level, wash the leaves, and serve one whole plant to each person. For a continuous crop, sow lettuce every two weeks up to the middle of July. There is no need to have large containers for lettuce: you may grow a good supply in a couple of window or railing boxes just 7 inches deep by 8 inches wide at the top. Use the same soil mix and fertilizer suggested for tomatoes.

Radishes, another vegetable useful in salads, should also be sown directly outside. Choose 'Saxa' or 'Cherry Belle'. These will grow rapidly, especially if your balcony gets plenty of sun, so do not be surprised if you harvest your first 'Saxa' radishes only three weeks after you sowed the seed. Make regular two-week sowings for a continuous crop.

Onions will add that bit of tang to your summer salads. Try onion 'sets', the tiny onion bulbs three-quarters of an inch in diameter grown especially to provide either tender green salad onions during the summer or larger cooking onions just before frost. Sets are available in early spring, usually boxed or bagged, from supermarkets, seed stores, or mail-order seed houses. The best varieties for balcony gardens are 'Yellow Ebenezer' or 'White Ebenezer'. Plant the onion bulbs 2 inches apart – 3 inches apart if you plan not to harvest them until the fall.

Cucumbers, too, are a useful ingredient in many salads. Three varieties in particular are suited to container growing. Two of them, 'Victory' and 'Triumph', are excellent for slicing. Start the seed indoors about May 1, using jiffy pots or planting strips so that the

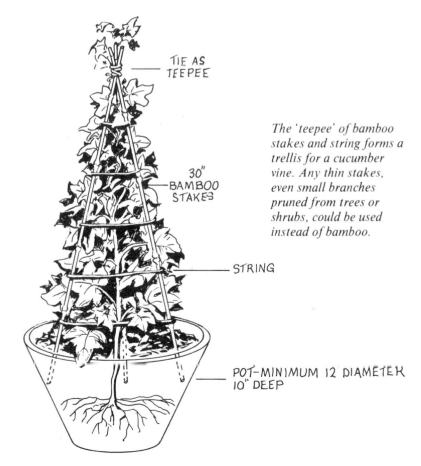

TIE AS TEEPEE

30" BAMBOO STAKES

STRING

POT—MINIMUM 12 DIAMETER 10" DEEP

The 'teepee' of bamboo stakes and string forms a trellis for a cucumber vine. Any thin stakes, even small branches pruned from trees or shrubs, could be used instead of bamboo.

plants do not suffer from transplant shock when they are moved outside. If you prefer to start the seed outside, wait until two weeks after the average last frost date for your area. Plant three or four plants (or thin out your seedlings to this number) in the centre of a container at least 12 inches in diameter and 10 inches deep. Insert three thin stakes (bamboo, perhaps) each about 3 feet long equidistant around the edge of the pot, and form a "teepee' by tying them together at the top. This open tent-like formation will provide a framework to which you can tie string, thus forming a trellis for the cucumber vines. Since both 'Victory' and 'Triumph' mature in just fifty days, you can make an additional sowing for a later crop two or three weeks after planting your first seeds. If it is small gherkins you want to grow, then 'Patio Pick' is the cucumber for you. It grows into a small plant not more than 30 inches tall, and several sowings may be made during the growing season.

More Root Vegetables

Leafy vegetables are not the only ones that will grow in containers: in addition to the root vegetables (radishes and onions) for salads that I have just mentioned, try carrots and beets, too. But, as in ground-level gardening, do not try to start your root crops indoors – sow them outdoors in containers as soon as the soil is workable. You may have to protect the sprouted seedlings on nights when light frosts are predicted, but you can easily do that by spreading a few layers of newspaper over the tops of the containers in the evening. Be sure you remember to remove the covering early the next morning. Since most root vegetables, such as beets, do not compete with leaf crops, such as lettuce, you might interplant some of each to save space.

If you like carrots, try the tiny fingerling gourmet types such as 'Sucram' or 'Baby Finger'. Sow the seed thinly, and thin out the seedlings just as the roots begin to develop. Do not throw away the thinnings: you will thoroughly enjoy their sweet flavour and tenderness while you wait for your main crop.

Some people like beets, especially in their salads, but dislike the way their dark-red colour transfers to the other ingredients. The answer to this problem is the relatively new 'Golden Beet', hybridized in Canada and now easily obtainable. Beets are, of course, a dual-purpose vegetable, since the tops (the beet greens) as well as the roots are edible. 'Golden Beet' is especially valuable since the tops are even more delicious to eat than spinach, and the orange-coloured roots are excellent either in salads or as a vegetable on their own – without the dark-red colour to spoil the look of the salad as a whole or of any other food on the same plate.

Vegetables: Plain or Exotic

Beans, too, will provide a plentiful crop grown in containers. 'Sprite' and 'Bush Blue Lake' will yield beans in slightly less than eight weeks after being planted, and if your favourites are Italian Romano or wax beans, try 'Bush Romano' or 'Honey Gold' bush wax beans. The Romano beans are famous for their distinctive flavour. Each 'Honey Gold' plant will yield twenty-four or more beans about 5 to 6 inches long.

You may be interested in the more unusual vegetables – and there is plenty of choice. 'Green Curled' endive, and 'Full Heart' escarole are interesting substitutes for lettuce, and although they take three to four weeks longer to mature than 'Buttercrunch' lettuce, they have a distinct flavour of their own. Seeds of these varieties should be sown directly outdoors from April 15 to June 30, with the date of last sowing about ninety days before the average date of the first frost in your area, to give the final crop time to mature.

Many Canadians are not even familiar with eggplant, that deep purple, almost black, cylindrical fruit (used as a vegetable) whose shape resembles a vegetable marrow. However, once you have savoured it, prepared as you would prepare vegetable marrow, you may well become an enthusiast. It is adaptable to container growing, and if you choose a variety such as 'T.S. Cross Hybrid' you will be able to pick the first almost round, deep-purple fruit, weighing about a pound, approximately nine weeks after setting out the plants. Eggplant should really be started from seed indoors, some time during March. The seed likes a very warm growing medium (over 80°F, 27°C) and, once it has germinated, a temperature of 72°F (22°C) is ideal for the seedlings. Since the plants are set back by cold weather they should remain indoors except on warm days until all danger of night temperatures below 45°F (7°C) is over.

If you want to be even more adventuresome, try Brussels sprouts, peas, and almost any other vegetable in the seed catalogue that interests you. For satisfactory results, though, be certain to follow the carefully developed seeding techniques given in the catalogue.

Herbs

The flavour of many vegetables is improved by the addition of herbs, which are becoming increasingly popular with ground-level and apartment gardeners alike. Herbs such as anise, borage, chives, dill, fennel, rosemary, sage, basil, sweet marjoram, summer savory, and tarragon may all be grown in small containers. Most of these, however, take a minimum of nine weeks to mature. If you wish to grow them, you should start the seeds indoors – either in late winter under a fluorescent fixture or in early spring on a bright window sill – so that established plants are ready to be set out in late May. Most department stores and seed supply outlets sell small and large herb starter kits which include individual containers, the seeds, and the necessary instructions – or you could order packets of seed from a mail-order seed house (most of them offer a collection of the popular types at a saving) and ,start them in your own containers. If it is too late or inconvenient to start seeds, herb plants are obtainable from various types of outlets. Be sure that all danger of frost is over before you put the plants outside.

Fruit Trees

Obvious additions to the balcony vegetable garden are some small fruits, perhaps even some tree fruits. Since fruit trees are not as hardy as the trees and shrubs discussed in Chapter 6, it is very difficult to get them to live through the winter in balcony containers. In fact, without all the protective measures detailed in that chapter, which include insulating the inside of the container with styrofoam and wrapping the outside with fiberglas insulation batts, your efforts to grow fruit will probably be unsuccessful. But if you are prepared to undertake these protective measures, along with the necessary spray schedules to combat insects and disease, dwarf apple trees (the most hardy of the fruit trees) in large containers on your balcony should grow well.

If you happen to read gardening magazines published for areas such as Boston and New York city, which have even milder weather than western New York state and southern Ontario, you may see a dwarf peach tree 'Bonanza' advertised as being ideally suited to container growing. Beware – this is not necessarily so for *your* region. Though this beautiful dwarf peach may be successfully grown in climates only very slightly milder than southern Ontario's, it does not winter north of the Great Lakes, and in a balcony container it will obviously require complete winter protection if it is to live from year to year.

Strawberries

Strawberries are the ideal small fruit to try on your balcony, since you can grow quite a number of plants in a relatively small space. Of the two methods most suited to balconies, the easiest is to use a conical aluminum planter, approximately 6 feet in diameter and 2 feet high, that is available from most mail-order seed houses. It is constructed of three corrugated aluminum rings of decreasing diameter that sit one on top of each other. Filled with soil or planting medium, the planter will hold about fifty strawberry plants. If you wish, you may combine a smaller number of strawberries with annual flowers or herbs, or with small vegetables such as radishes or lettuce. The varieties of strawberry best suited to these planters are the so-called ever-bearing types such as 'Chief Bemidji', 'Autumn Beauty', and

An aluminum conical planter can be used for growing small annuals such as portulaca, lobelia, sweet alyssum, French marigolds, and zinnias, as well as small vegetables. Of course it can be used exclusively for strawberries, or for strawberries combined with some of the other suggested plants.

'Jumbo', which you can buy as small plants in early spring. 'Chief Bemidji' and 'Autumn Beauty' produce their first fruit in June, and continue to give fruit throughout the summer and until frost. 'Jumbo' bears a mid-season crop only, but is a heavy producer of large, luscious berries. Strawberries planted in a conical planter should be protected in winter. Cover the entire planter with batts of fiberglas insulation, or with straw weighted down so that it does not blow away.

The second method of growing strawberries on your balcony is to use a homemade strawberry barrel. The barrel provides an attractive container for growing up to fifty strawberry plants in a circular area only 3 feet in diameter – but to build one involves a little work on your part. Start by looking for a suitable used barrel; any size will do, from small nail kegs to the large 45-gallon wooden barrels still occasionally used for some foods. It is best not to select barrels that have been used for brine, vinegar, or paint, because these often contain traces of toxic substances that may be injurious. Good sources for these barrels are perhaps a local winemaker's supply store, the local junk dumps, or even a country store or auction.

To prepare your barrel as a planter, begin by boring several 1½-inch holes in the base, for drainage. Then attach roller-skate wheels, or casters designed for office chairs, either to a separate base on which the barrel will stand (being careful not to block the drainage holes) or directly to the bottom of the barrel. It is important that the barrel be easy to move, since it must be turned forty-five degrees each day so that all the plants receive their quota of light.

Next, the holes for the individual plants must be marked. These should be 2 inches in diameter. The holes should not be closer together than 6 inches, and need not be farther apart than 10 inches; the spacing will depend on the position of the metal hoops. The best plan is to mark the first row of holes immediately below the upper hoop or hoops, spacing them from 6 to 8 inches apart at an equal distance from each other all around the barrel. Then mark the next row of holes, about 6 inches further down the barrel and midway between each two of the holes in the upper row. In the next row, the holes should be immediately below those in the first row, creating a staggered effect. The last row should be marked no closer than 6 inches from the bottom of the barrel. You will need an expansion bit for your brace to bore the 2-inch holes.

Before filling your barrel with soil, put in large pieces of old broken flowerpots or large stones – or even a piece of window screening – over the drainage holes to prevent the soil from falling through. Then put about 3 or 4 inches of coarse gravel, stones, perlite, or similar drainage material at the bottom. At this point, you should leave space for a drainage core up through the centre of the barrel. The base of this core can be a 4- or 5-inch clay flowerpot with its bottom knocked out, placed upside-down on top of the layer of drainage material. The rest of the core may be made of old window screening, newspaper, or any porous, semi-durable, flat material that will bend. Roll it up to make a tube 4 inches in diameter, the same height as the barrel.

The soil mix for strawberries, or any other plants to be grown in your barrel, should contain liberal amounts of peat moss or leaf mould (or both), as well as sand. A mixture of a third each of peat moss, sharp sand, and good garden loam is ideal. Before you begin to fill the barrel with soil, place the tubular central core over the upside-down flowerpot and have someone hold it in the centre of the

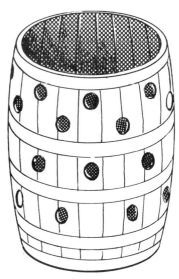

(2) *Settling the soil at the three-quarters full level, before the final layer is added. Note the position of the flowerpot.*

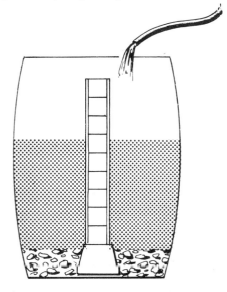

(1) *The empty barrel showing holes bored.*

A BARREL OF STRAWBERRIES

barrel. Then fill the tubular core a quarter of the way up with loose drainage material. Next, fill the rest of the barrel with the soil mix to the same level as the filling in the central core. Water this soil thoroughly to settle it, and push it well down to force out all the air pockets – this is very important. Wait at least half an hour before filling the central core to the halfway point with the same drainage material; then fill the rest of the barrel halfway with more of the soil mix. Soak this well, too, and wait again before proceeding in two similar steps to fill the top half of the barrel.

At the top of the central core, place a second flowerpot, right side up and with its bottom knocked out, inside the newspaper tube. Fill the central core right up to the top of this pot, which should be an inch above the soil level in the barrel.

Once the barrel is filled, you can put in the plants, each with its crown at the soil edge and level with the inner edge of the barrel. The number of plants will depend on the size of your barrel and the

(3) The barrel filled with soil and ready to be planted.

(4) The central core filled with fine gravel.

(5) The planted barrel, showing the plant crown even with the rim of the hole.

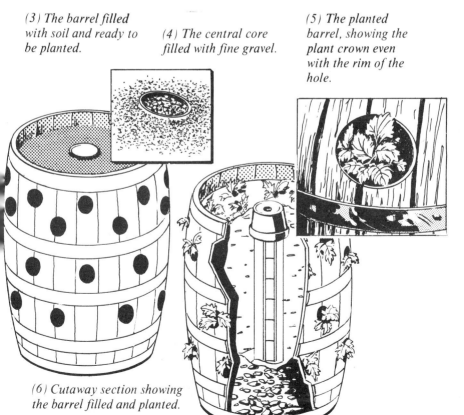

(6) Cutaway section showing the barrel filled and planted.

position of the hoops, but a large 45-gallon barrel should take four rows of eight to ten holes each, giving a total of thirty-two to forty planting holes; in addition, the top of the barrel will have space for another eight or ten plants, for a total of fifty plants in one barrel.

Maintenance of barrel and contents is simple. Water the planted barrel through the central core; and in addition, to make sure that the plants growing at the top receive their share, pour water directly onto the top surface. Any flowers that are produced on the strawberry plants during the first month should be removed, in order to give the plants an opportunity to get established. Later in the year the plants will produce runners, and these, too, should be removed to encourage the formation of multiple crowns and thus fill the 2-inch holes. Winter protection, similar to that described for the conical planter, will be necessary for your strawberry barrel if you wish to keep the plants alive for the next season. Provided the protection is adequate, the plants should thrive for three or four years without having to be replaced.

Your strawberry barrel will serve as a good home for almost any variety of strawberries, but if you are not particularly interested in growing strawberries at all, the small vegetables suggested earlier for the conical planter are also ideal for a barrel, and you could also grow annual flowers such as dwarf snapdragons, lobelia, sweet alyssum, and impatiens, and trailing plants such as German ivy. You need not provide winter protection for these annual plants, since new ones have to be put in each year.

No matter what you plant in your barrel, a liquid fertilizer instead of plain water once a month is necessary. Since both fruit and flowers are encouraged by a fertilizer high in phosphate, a liquid plant food with a formula similar to 15-30-15 will suit almost any plants in your barrel.

Trees and Shrubs for Your Balcony

Until recently, professional horticulturists believed that only a very few species of shrubs and dwarf trees could live in containers for a succession of winters. As we shall see in this chapter, there is now no need to accept severe restrictions on the choice of plants for balconies. Through limited, unrelated, and sometimes unintentional tests, it is known that a much wider range of trees and shrubs than traditionally expected can be successfully grown in containers. Apartment gardeners who wish to grow plants other than common annuals, for years the standard recommendation of the Canadian horticultural trade, will benefit from some of today's newer theories. The suggestions in this chapter are really only a beginning; really only a base from which the interested apartment gardener may begin to experiment, with results that he or she will be able to enjoy through the balcony's glass doors and windows both summer and winter.

A gardener in southern Ontario (or in an area with a similar climate) looking for a tree able to live through the winters in a container may even today be advised by nurserymen and garden centre staff to plant a Japanese yew or Korean box evergreen. The truth is that while such plants do look attractive in containers, chiefly because of their statuesque habit, they often suffer badly over winter, and though they may survive, tend to look so ragged and burned by the time spring comes that they are often replaced.

Unfortunately, our knowledge of gardening practices built up during the past decade of rapid expansion in the horticultural industry in

Canada does not include information about growing trees in containers. Gardeners have therefore been almost entirely deprived of advice on how to grow deciduous trees (those that lose their leaves in winter) and conifers (needle-bearing trees usually called evergreens, with foliage remaining green all year) on their balconies.

The Plant Hardiness Zone Map

We are not without some guidance, however, to help us decide which plants to grow. In 1967, the federal Department of Agriculture (now called Agriculture Canada) released its new and carefully researched Canadian Plant Hardiness Zone Map. This map divides the country into nine zones of plant hardiness and eighteen sub-zones – the milder the climate the higher the number. Obviously a larger variety of plants, especially those susceptible to frost damage, survive in the higher-numbered zones, whereas the low-numbered zones support only the hardiest plants, those able to withstand prolonged frozen soil and persistent chilling winds. If you have visited any of the urban centres in the three colder zones (for example, Fort Frances, Ontario; Baie-Comeau, Quebec; or Edmonton, Alberta) you may have noticed that the plants, especially the trees, are much more limited in species and number than they are in the milder zones. No oaks, beeches, magnolias, honey-locusts, catalpas, or sugar maples grow in the northerly zones. The trees that do survive are much shorter in height than those of the same variety in more southerly areas; even evergreen trees grow more slowly in colder climates and never achieve the great heights of the ones on the coast of British Columbia or the large sizes of those in southern Ontario and Quebec and milder parts of the Atlantic Provinces.

The main reason put forward by nurserymen for suggesting such a small range of plants for containers was that the soil in a small container freezes much more solidly than does a large quantity of earth in a ground-level garden, and thus most plants cannot survive. We can agree with this theory, and should also remember that in general, the soil in the more northerly areas freezes harder and for longer periods than it does farther south – one of the reasons why not many trees grow in the north or at higher altitudes. But some hardy species do thrive. Why not try some of these in containers? Though Canadian research has been lacking in this important subject, isolated individual experiments have been carried out.

Here is a list of seventy-five Canadian cities and towns, together with the zone in which each is located, so that you may compare your climate with the climates mentioned in the book.

Agassiz, B.C.	8a	Parry Sound, Ont.	5a
Banff, Alta.	1b	Pembroke, Ont.	4b
Barrie, Ont.	5a	Peterborough, Ont.	5b
Brandon, Man.	2b	Portage la Prairie, Man.	3a
Calgary, Alta.	3a	Powell River, B.C.	9a
Campbellton, N.B.	4b	Prince Albert, Sask.	1b
Chatham, Ont.	7a	Prince George, B.C.	3a
Charlottetown, P.E.I.	5b	Prince Rupert, B.C.	8a
Chicoutimi, P.Q.	3b	Princeton, B.C.	3a
Corner Brook, Nfld.	4b	Quebec City, P.Q.	4b
Cornwall, Ont.	5b	Red Lake, Ont.	2b
Dawson Creek, B.C.	2a	Regina, Sask.	2b
Edmonton, Alta.	3a	Revelstoke, B.C.	6a
Edson, Alta.	2a	Sarnia, Ont.	6b
Flin Flon, Man.	1b	Saskatoon, Sask.	2b
Fredericton, N.B.	5a	Sault Ste. Marie, Ont.	4b
Golden, B.C.	3a	Sept Iles, P.Q.	3a
Grand Bank, Nfld.	6a	Sherbrooke, P.Q.	4a
Grande Prairie, Alta.	2a	St. John's, Nfld.	5b
Halifax, N.S.	6a	Swift Current, Sask.	3a
Hamilton, Ont.	6b	The Pas, Man.	1b
Kamloops, B.C.	6a	Thunder Bay, Ont.	3a
Kapuskasing, Ont.	2a	Timiskaming, Ont.	3a
Kelowna, B.C.	6a	Timmins, Ont.	1b
Kenora, Ont.	3a	Toronto, Ont.	6a
Kimberley, B.C.	3a	Trail, B.C.	7a
Kitchener, Ont.	6a	Trois Rivières, P.Q.	4b
Lacombe, Alta.	2a	Vancouver, B.C.	8b
Lethbridge, Alta.	3a	Vermilion, Alta.	2a
London, Ont.	6b	Vernon, B.C.	6a
Lytton, B.C.	7a	Victoria, B.C.	8b
Moncton, N.B.	5a	Welland, Ont.	6b
Montreal, P.Q.	5b	Weyburn, Sask.	2b
Morden, Man.	3b	Windsor, Ont.	7a
New Liskeard, Ont.	3a	Winnipeg, Man.	3a
Niagara Falls, Ont.	7a	Yarmouth, N.S.	6b
Ottawa, Ont.	5a	Yorkton, Sask.	2a
Owen Sound, Ont.	5b		

Throughout this book, climates are compared with southern Ontario, which is in zone 6a or 6b. Zone 6b is slightly milder than zone 6a.

A Case Study

When it was built in the early 1960s, a fifth-floor balcony of a Toronto office building included two medium-sized plant containers. Because the balcony faced east and Japanese yews grow well in shade, nurserymen recommended that traditional yew as a satisfactory evergreen for these containers. But the trees could not withstand the winter, and had to be replaced each spring for several years.

The building managers finally grew tired of the continual expense and labour, and asked me what I thought they should plant instead. They specified a plant about 3 feet tall that would still be alive after the gruelling winter. I explained that I was certain it was more important to plant an extremely hardy small tree or shrub than one tolerant of the shady easterly exposure. I also said that in my opinion the amount of light available five storeys up on an easterly exposure would probably be almost as much as is normally found facing west at ground level.

The building managers accepted my advice and decided that they did not necessarily need evergreens, since the balcony was not used during the winter. Jointly, we agreed that flowers in spring or early summer would be more valuable, and for each container chose a weeping peashrub (*Caragana arborescens* 'Pendula'), a small-leaved shrub whose branches hang down from a 4-foot stem. As the plant matures, the number of branches increases but its basic height does not, because of its weeping habit. The plant is extremely hardy, growing well in zones 2 to 9. It is a close relative of the Siberian peashrub (*Caragana arborescens*), well known on the prairies as a hedgerow or windbreak. Attractive bright-yellow flowers resembling those of sweet peas appear in early summer, followed by small seed pods. The two trees are still in the same containers today; they have been growing on that fifth-floor balcony for ten years!

Before continuing this chapter, I should emphasize that there has been no basic research into growing trees and shrubs in containers, and that you might not be able to duplicate exactly the results of some of the experiments I describe, which have taken place mainly in southern Ontario (zone 5 and 6). Your success will depend a good deal on your climate. Toronto, for example, is milder than Montreal and a great deal milder than Ottawa. In cities that have extremely cold winters, such as Ottawa, also Winnipeg and other prairie cities,

The weeping peashrub is a small hardy tree suited to almost any balcony.

3½′

it may not be possible to grow all the plants I suggest. But if the climate where you live is at all similar to that of southern Ontario, it would be worth your while at least to try.

Small deciduous trees such as the weeping peashrub are not the only taller-growing permanent plants that may be tried in balcony containers. Once you have had a garden on your balcony for a year or two, you will probably want to begin experimenting yourself with the hardier evergreen trees (conifers) as well as with some of the hardy deciduous shrubs.

Evergreens

Here are a few of the evergreen varieties you may wish to try, either in your floor garden or in larger containers on the balcony. Do not be too concerned about the amount of light or sun available to them, unless your balcony is particularly sunny or remains constantly in deep shade. Junipers prefer bright locations; the other evergreens suggested here should thrive in any exposure. Since most ornamental evergreens grow in either upright or spreading forms, I shall deal with them under these two headings.

Hardy Spreading and Mound-like Evergreens

The most useful of the spreading evergreens are a number of the junipers, because their ultimate height and spread in a container is not likely to exceed three or four feet. The colour of the foliage varies according to the variety and, in some species, with the changing of the seasons.

The lowest spreading variety is repanda juniper (*Juniperus communis* 'Repanda'), growing to a height of only a few inches and hugging the soil. It is green in colour. Similar in habit, but blue, particularly in the spring, is blue acres juniper (*Juniperus horizontalis* 'Blue Acres'). The walkegan juniper (*Juniperus horizontalis* 'Douglasii') is a deep steel blue, the colour becoming deep purple for the entire winter season. The change in colour to purple for the winter is even more evident in the slightly taller and bushier Andorra juniper (*Juniperus horizontalis* 'Plumosa'), which is green through spring, summer, and early autumn.

Introduced from Beaverlodge, Alberta (zone 2), the dark-green wapiti juniper (*Juniperus horizontalis* 'Wapiti') starts by growing upright but soon flattens out to become a vigorous spreader. Extending to a saucer shape, the medium-green branches of the Arcadia juniper (*Juniperus sabina* 'Arcadia') quickly grow to a maximum of 18 inches high. An old standby, the golden pfitzer juniper (*Juniperus chinensis* 'Pfitzeriana Aurea'), provided it receives three or four hours of sunlight each day, is an interesting yellow colour – particularly the new spring foliage. Finally one of my favourites, a plant that will take several years to reach a height and spread of 2 or 3 feet: the maney juniper (*Juniperus chinensis* 'Maney'). It remains a delightful silver-grey colour throughout the year, and while not quite as hardy in the north as the golden pfitzer, should grow well in a container given some protection from winter winds.

There are still other spreading or mound-like evergreens, some of which may be familiar to you, suitable for apartment gardens. Almost everyone knows the beautiful blue spruce (see the following section about upright evergreens) so common along our suburban streets. There is now a dwarf, compact form, with the same colourful light-blue needles all year round. The globe blue spruce (*Picea pungens*

Junipers of various forms are hardy; they should grow on most balconies that are bright during the day, in climates similar to those of southern Ontario, the Atlantic Provinces, and British Columbia. Even in colder areas they may be grown successfully with little or no winter protection. From left to right: Andorra, maney, and skyrocket varieties.

MANEY JUNIPER

ANDORRA JUNIPER

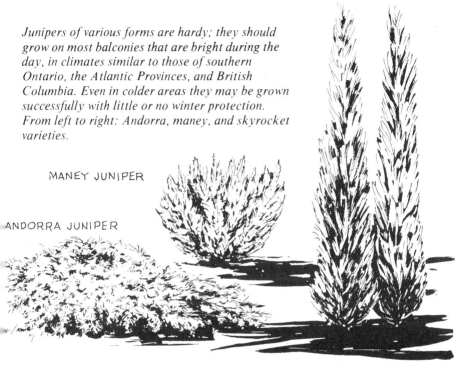

'Globosa') is equally hardy and will withstand many winters in a container on a balcony; it provides an exciting accent of colour even in winter. Also well known is the mugho pine (*Pinus mugo mugo*), the dwarf pine which makes an ideal centre for a medium-sized container, perhaps surrounded by annual or perennial flowers. To keep this pine dwarf and mound shaped, you should pinch off half to two-thirds of all the finger-like new growths produced by the middle of June each year.

True cedars, which belong to the botanical genus *Cedrus*, do not grow in eastern Canada, though they have been successfully introduced into the milder coastal regions of British Columbia. The trees we call 'cedars' are really arbor-vitae of the genus *Thuja*, and many varieties can be successfully grown in balcony gardens. One that thrives in containers is the globe cedar (*Thuja occidentalis* 'Woodwardii'). The plant is well named, for it forms a round ball without any pruning.

Two other interesting and unusual dwarf plants are not needle evergreens but broadleaf evergreens. Broadleaf evergreens retain their

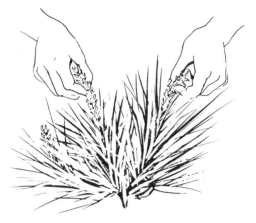

*In mid-June,
pinch off half to
two-thirds of the
new growth of
your mugho pine
– like this.*

flat leaves all year (rhododendrons are perhaps the most familiar example). Some plants of this type that like growing in balcony containers are pachystima (*Pachistima canbyi*) and rose daphne (*Daphne cneorum*). Pachystima is 6 to 12 inches tall with narrow, pointed, flat leaves that are dark green all year; rose daphne, about the same height, becomes covered in tiny rose-pink flowers each May, and for the remainder of the year has light-green foliage.

Hardy Upright Evergreens

Unlike my suggested dwarf and mound-like evergreens, most of the following upright varieties that I recommend to you for your balcony normally grow larger, but if they are planted in containers or floor gardens will remain relatively small for many years because their root growth is restricted.

The smallest of the upright-growing evergreens is, without doubt, the bristlecone pine (*Pinus aristata*). This plant will seldom, even in twenty years, exceed 10 feet in height under ideal growing conditions, so if it is in a container do not expect your 6-inch nursery plant to be more than a foot tall even after many growing seasons. A second slow-growing upright evergreen, though suitable for containers on east and north exposures only, is the dwarf Alberta spruce (*Picea glauca albertiana* 'Conica'). Though hardy in zones 4 to 9, the soft needles of this attractive little tree are easily burned by the winter sun and wind. Therefore, if you grow it on a south, southwest, or west balcony, be sure to wrap the plant loosely with burlap or other cloth (not plastic) during January to March each year. The dwarf Alberta spruce has light-green needles half an inch long and grows in a compact, conical shape. The only other hardy upright evergreen that can be considered truly dwarf is the dwarf Scots pine (*Pinus sylvestris* 'Watereri'), which will probably not exceed 5 or 6 feet after ten or twelve years in a container. This plant has dark-green, almost blue-green, needles, similar to those on the Scots pines normally used as Christmas trees. It grows in a somewhat globular shape, almost as wide as it is tall.

Of the other taller evergreens that I suggest you might consider for container or floor garden planting on a balcony, two are junipers – named blue heaven (*Juniperus scopulorum* 'Blue Heaven') and sky-rocket (*Juniperus virginiana* 'Skyrocket'). Both are conical, though skyrocket is much the thinner of the two. Blue heaven is a delightful mid-blue, while skyrocket is medium-green to grey-blue.

Four well-known spruce trees, two of which are commonly used for timber, are extremely hardy and suitable for container growing. These are the Norway spruce (*Picea abies*), white spruce (*Picea glauca*), Colorado spruce (*Picea pungens*), and Koster blue spruce (*Picea pungens* 'Koster'). All of these grow to heights of 50 to 70 feet ornamentally, and even taller in the forest, but if planted in containers

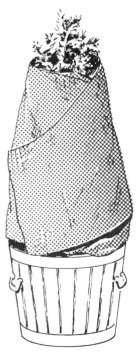

You will have greater success in keeping your dwarf Alberta spruce from year to year if you wrap it with burlap in late December and leave it protected in this way until early April. If the plant is in the shade for the entire winter, though, the wrapping should not be necessary. One more strip of burlap around the top of this plant would complete the wrapping.

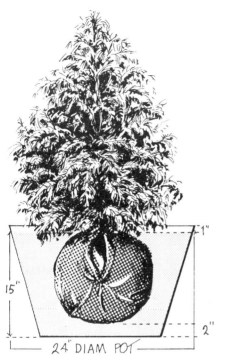

15"

1"

2"

24" DIAM POT

A balled and burlapped evergreen, as shown here, should be planted in a container with a diameter at least 12 inches greater than the diameter of the soil ball. Partly fill the container with soil, leaving a hole in which the evergreen will sit so that the top of the ball will be even with the final level of soil in the container. Place the evergreen in the container and fill in the remainder of the space with soil, being careful to compact it hard around the soil ball. The burlap need not be removed, but if you wish you may cut it once the evergreen is planted, and fold down the corners into the surrounding soil. If the soil ball is wrapped in plastic burlap, this should be removed entirely. Water the plant well, and give a liquid fertilizer (30-15-15) to both the foliage and the soil.

when they are only 2 or 3 feet high, will remain under 5 feet for many years. The white spruce has medium-green, somewhat bluish needles half an inch long; the Norway's dark-green needles are similar but its growth habit is more picturesque; the Colorado's needles are much longer and are green in colour, while the Koster has long, light-blue needles that retain their blue tinge throughout the year.

One other tall, slow-growing evergreen that is hardy and thus suited to container growing is the Swiss stone pine (*Pinus cembra*). This plant grows in an extremely narrow columnar form that makes an ideal centre for a large container of flowers.

Planting Evergreens in Containers

All these evergreens need a minimum soil depth of 12 inches, though a depth of 15 inches is desirable. You should plant them in floor-level containers or floor gardens. Evergreens all like a soil with plenty of organic matter, so either a Cornell mix (see p. 13) or a third each of garden loam, peat moss (or other organic material such as leaf mould or cattle manure), and sand is good for them.

Ideally, the evergreens should be planted between the end of April and the beginning of June, or from the beginning of July until the middle of the month, provided that the temperature is not consistently over 75°F (24°C). The very best time to plant is early May. Even though your nurseryman may tell you that evergreens may be planted in September, before doing so make certain that he, as supplier, will be willing to replace them should they die during the winter. Many garden centres have a policy of not extending their normal guarantee to plants, particularly evergreens, if they are to be planted in containers.

How Evergreens Are Sold

Because evergreens are constantly giving off moisture through their needles, their roots should be constantly in touch with moist soil. Unlike deciduous trees and shrubs, which are dormant and without leaves from late fall to early spring and can therefore be sold with bare roots, evergreens must of course be dug with a full growth of needles. They must be sold complete with a ball of soil containing the roots, in a form known as 'balled and burlapped'.

When you are looking for an evergreen, it is just as important to buy one with a good solid soil ball as with attractive, healthy branches and needles. Once you have decided on the variety, be sure to look through the garden centre's supply for the one plant with the best combination of good foliage and large, solid (not loose or damaged) soil ball.

Caring for Evergreens

Evergreens require plenty of water, and during hot days, even if the humidity is high, they will appreciate a regular dousing that reaches all their needles. This watering takes the place of the rinsing they would normally get from the rain if they were growing in a garden. Most balconies remain untouched by rainfall, except perhaps during driving rainstorms, and the plants miss having their foliage regularly cleansed by the rain. Evergreens should be fertilized every thirty days from early spring until mid-August; use a liquid fertilizer with an analysis of 30-10-10, or a formula similar to that.

It is especially important that by the time the winter freeze-up arrives, evergreens on balconies be well moistened. You should water them regularly immediately before freeze-up – a time when you might ordinarily tend to think that watering is unnecessary. Evergreens, because they retain their needles throughout the year, continue to transpire a small amount of moisture through their leaves (needles) during the winter. Only if a plant has an adequate supply of moisture available at its roots to replace what is transpired will it have a reasonable chance of coming through the winter unscathed.

Hardy Deciduous Trees

As I mentioned at the beginning of this chapter, two weeping peashrubs have been thriving in containers on a fifth-floor Toronto suburban balcony for about ten years. However, if my description of the weeping peashrub does not appeal to you, do not be concerned; many other small trees and shrubs, though they lose their leaves for the winter, can provide you with year-round interest if planted on a balcony. Unless your balcony is consistently shaded by an adjacent structure, all the following suggested deciduous trees should thrive regardless of which direction your balcony faces.

Here are the names of a few other deciduous trees, including dwarf trees, for balcony gardens. Some of the dwarf varieties are really shrubs either budded or grafted onto 4- or 5-foot stems; these are known as 'standards'.

The only tree in my selection that does not have a noticeable flower is the grey birch (*Betula populifolia*). This is one of the birches with white peeling bark. It does not grow as tall as most varieties of birch, but if you plan to try one, buy the smallest size available (5 feet) and keep it pruned to that size. The tree will require a deeper than average container, certainly no shallower than 18 inches.

Of the flowering trees, the crabapples are amongst the most popular with ground-level gardeners. Several of the varieties, because of their particular hardiness and dwarf nature, seem to be ideal for containers. The Almey crabapple (*Malus* 'Almey'), with its cherry-red flowers, green foliage, and persistent, small, orange fruits, has been a favourite all across Canada for many years. A crabapple grown mainly for the colour of its foliage is Royalty (*Malus* 'Royalty'), which has shiny maroon leaves throughout the season and red flowers in the spring. A different genus of shrub, also with maroon foliage

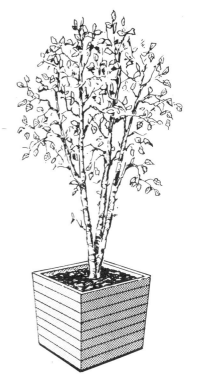

White birch – also known as paper birch – thrive in large containers. Circular containers should have a minimum diameter of 30 inches; rectangular containers should have sides not less than 24 inches long.

that lasts well all season, is the purple leaf sand cherry (*Prunus cistena*). This little tree has tiny white flowers in the spring, though it is grown mainly for the colour and lasting quality of its leaves.

Two other ornamental cherries which are hardy and suitable for containers are the choke cherry (*Prunus maackii*) with its clusters of small white flowers and golden-coloured bark that peels rather like birchbark, and the Manchu cherry (*Prunus tomentosa* standard), one of the standard shrubs. Manchu cherry is the hardiest of all the cherries. It bears pink flowers which lighten to white before falling, and are followed in late summer by edible red cherries. A close relative of these cherries is the flowering almond (*Prunus triloba* 'Multiplex'), a standard shrub noted for a proliferation of beautiful pink, fully-double flowers in early spring before the foliage appears. Unfortunately, the various species of flowering almond are prone to disease and all are short-lived.

One of the first flowering trees to bloom in the spring is the Saskatoon berry (*Amelanchier alnifolia*), which produces tiny white flowers followed in late summer by purple berries that make superb pie. Another tree that flowers early is the toba hawthorn (*Crataegus mor-*

denensis 'Toba'), which was developed in Morden, Manitoba. Its pinkish flowers, which come out in June, fade to white before falling. They are followed in late summer by red fruits that remain on the tree into winter.

Also well suited to container planting are the French hybrid lilacs (*Syringa vulgaris*, French hybrids), which flower in late May and are available in several varieties and colours as standards. In addition to these, you might consider the Japanese tree lilac (*Syringa amurensis japonica*); it flowers about two weeks later than the French hybrids, producing trusses of creamy-white bloom.

Another standard shrub that could become popular for container planting is the European snowball (*Viburnum opulus* 'Roseum'). Its white flowers in June are produced in large ball-shaped heads, thus its common name 'snowball'. In autumn, the colour of its foliage is brilliant yellow and orange.

Last, but as always not least, is a close relative of the weeping peashrub described earlier. The globe Siberian peashrub (*Caragana arborescens*, clipped globe) is really a shrub caragana grafted onto a 4-foot stem and usually kept clipped in the shape of a globe, though it can of course also be clipped in any other shape, or left unclipped.

Deciduous Shrubs that Branch from the Ground

We have just been discussing deciduous trees and some of the taller deciduous shrubs. But there will doubtless be readers who, though they want to try a deciduous plant rather than an evergreen for their

European snowball, a hardy shrub easily identified by its large round clusters of white flowers, may eventually grow to a height of 10 feet.

balconies, will prefer a lower-growing shrub that branches from the ground rather than a plant growing on a 4- to 6-foot stem. Most of the plants in the previous section are also available as shrubs branching from the ground. In order not to be repetitive, I shall omit from this section the plants just listed as tree or standard forms; nevertheless, you might consider them, too, before you make your choice. Many shrubs are not available as standards or trees, and I have chosen the best examples of these. The direction your balcony faces should not prevent you from growing any shrub you choose, unless the balcony is always in the shade of a nearby taller structure. If it is, silverleaf dogwood, Annabelle hydrangea, and false spirea are certain to perform well, but you might also try some of the others mentioned in the remainder of this section.

Only about half the deciduous shrubs I think worth trying as container plants on balconies are grown specifically for their flowers; the rest are valued for other features – foliage colour or texture, fruit colour or autumn colouration. Among the best of the shrubs for foliage colour alone are silverleaf dogwood (*Cornus alba* 'Elegantissima'), Russian olive (*Elaeagnus angustifolia*), sea-buckthorn (*Hippophae rhamnoides*), golden ninebark (*Physocarpus opulifolius* 'Luteus'), and buffalo berry *(Shepherdia argentea)*. Russian olive, sea-buckthorn, and buffalo berry all have silver-coloured foliage. Russian olive is a reliable and hardy shrub with its cool-looking silver foliage throughout the season and peeling bark in winter. Sea-buckthorn has orange fruit in the fall, and gives a brilliant splash of colour if several plants are set in a group. Buffalo berry produces red fruit in the fall, and several plants together give a cheerful mass of colour.

Golden ninebark, as its name implies, displays yellow foliage that lasts all season. It has small, light-pink flowers in June and red pods in the autumn. Silverleaf dogwood, colourful throughout the year, should become as popular with apartment gardeners as it is already with ground-level gardeners. Though the flowers are insignificant, the foliage is a variegated silvery-white and green, with each leaf slightly different from the next, an attractive effect that lasts all season whether the plant grows in sun or in shade. Then, after the leaves have fallen, the dark-red stems remain to brighten even a dreary winter's day.

If you have enough space to plant several bayberry (*Myrica pensylvanica*) shrubs, you will find that they produce grey waxy fruits, from which you might be able to make your own version of the popular

Cutleaf smooth sumac is an unusual shrub whose finely cut foliage and, in autumn, scarlet leaves and fruit, are particularly attractive.

scented candles! If you wish to grow a shrub simply for the texture of its foliage, be sure to consider cutleaf smooth sumac (*Rhus glabra* 'Laciniata'). In the fall, this sumac produces scarlet fruiting bodies which compete for attention with the brilliant colour assumed by the leaves at that time of year.

Flowering Shrubs

The remainder of my suggested deciduous shrubs consist of those which have noticeable flowers for periods of a few days to several weeks, and the shrubs I refer to in this section are grown mainly for their pleasing flowers. I shall begin with those that bloom earliest and progress to those that bloom later in the season.

The earliest of the hardy flowering shrubs to flower is the Saskatoon berry, mentioned in the section on hardy deciduous trees (p. 82). Another very early shrub is the Manchu cherry, also noted in that section.

A number of the shrubs that bloom in June can be expected to perform well if they are planted in containers. The honeysuckles (*Lonicera*) are a diverse group of shrubs, most of them blooming in late May and early June. Their tubular-shaped flowers vary in colour from creamy white through the various shades of pink to deep red, and most have red or bluish-black fruits in late summer. Blooming just slightly later than the French hybrid lilacs is the beautiful dwarf lilac (*Syringa velutina*), which grows into a thick bush only a few feet tall. Also in June, the cutleaf peashrub (*Caragana arborescens* 'Lorbergii') is in bloom with its small yellow flowers. This peashrub is different from the two varieties I mentioned earlier, the Siberian and the globe Siberian peashrub, in that its foliage is much more finely divided, making it appear more delicately attractive.

The high-bush cranberry (*Viburnum trilobum*) has white flowers in June, but is really grown primarily for its clusters of edible red berries in late summer. The spireas are a large group of shrubs varying greatly in appearance. The variety summersnow (*Spiraea* 'Summersnow'), for instance, bears flat heads of white flowers on 2-foot stems throughout June, July, and August; another variety of about the same height is Anthony Waterer (*Spiraea bumalda* 'Anthony Waterer') – but there the similarity ends; it has impressive cerise-red flowers in July, and the bloom will often continue in September, if the dead flower heads are pruned away.

Other flowering shrubs that bloom in July are false spirea (*Sorbaria sorbifolia*), which bears long pointed clusters of creamy-white flowers over a period of three to four weeks, and the Annabelle hydrangea (*Hydrangea arborescens* 'Annabelle'), a showy plant with white flowers borne in large round heads that turn a bronze shade and last right through the winter. Finally, consider also a dwarf shrub which bears prolifically through much of the summer – goldfinger cinquefoil (*Potentilla parvifolia* 'Goldfinger'). The flowers are golden yellow and about an inch in diameter. In winter, the foliage is slow to drop and, if the plant is growing close to the railing, it catches and holds the snow in an attractive manner.

Planting Deciduous Trees and Shrubs in Containers

Deciduous trees and shrubs are sold in a dormant state in the spring, before the new leaves have come out. Most of them have bare roots – that is, they are without a soil ball around their roots. In this dormant state, the trees and shrubs often look dead, but those new to gardening should not be deceived by the apparent lack of vitality.

The plants should be installed in their containers as soon as you receive them, and if they arrive from the nursery packed with moist, loose wood shavings, these must be discarded. When you plant the shrub or tree, do not place it any deeper than the depth at which it was growing in the nursery – the previous soil level is usually indicated by a slight change in colouration on the bark of the main stem.

Cut off any broken or damaged roots (do not be afraid to be ruthless), as these will be no use to the plant in getting established. Use the same soil mix as described for evergreens earlier in this chapter (p. 80).

The method of planting is simple. Spread out the roots in a hole deep enough and wide enough to accommodate them all without crowding, and as you fill in the hole with soil, tamp it solidly down with the heel of your shoe to eliminate any damaging air pockets around the roots.

Once the tree or shrub is planted, it should be pruned back, unless this is done for you by the nurseryman at the time you buy it. Depending on how much root was damaged and removed, cut back the branches to about half or a third of their original length. The more spindly and thin branches should be removed entirely. A few of the standard trees I have suggested will come balled and burlapped in

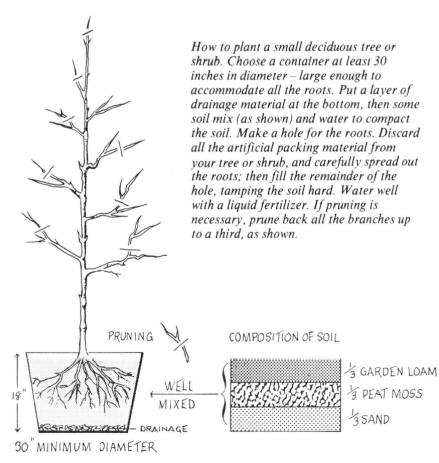

How to plant a small deciduous tree or shrub. Choose a container at least 30 inches in diameter – large enough to accommodate all the roots. Put a layer of drainage material at the bottom, then some soil mix (as shown) and water to compact the soil. Make a hole for the roots. Discard all the artificial packing material from your tree or shrub, and carefully spread out the roots; then fill the remainder of the hole, tamping the soil hard. Water well with a liquid fertilizer. If pruning is necessary, prune back all the branches up to a third, as shown.

PRUNING

COMPOSITION OF SOIL

WELL
MIXED

⅓ GARDEN LOAM
⅓ PEAT MOSS
⅓ SAND

18"

DRAINAGE

30" MINIMUM DIAMETER

the same manner as evergreens: these need not be trimmed back when you plant them.

After the trees or shrubs have been planted in their containers, give them enough water to soak the soil until it runs out of the drainage holes or, if there are no drainage holes, until the soil is moistened completely. Ideally, the first watering should contain an application of a starter fertilizer (the usual analysis is 10-45-15), which is specially formulated to encourage root development. This type of fertilizer is readily available, and a container of it is worth the small investment.

How to Tell if Your Shrub or Tree Is Alive

It is quite simple to decide whether an evergreen is alive or not: green foliage indicates a living plant, brown or red needles covering the entire plant mean that it has died. Look especially carefully at your tree or shrub at the time you plant it, as well as early the next spring after it has spent the winter in its balcony container.

Although it is not so immediately obvious whether a dormant and leafless deciduous tree or shrub is dead or not, there is a simple method of finding out. Lightly scrape the bark of one of the main branches or stems with your fingernail and note the condition and colour of the layer of tissue under the thin bark. The tissue of a live and healthy plant will be moist and bright green, that of a dead plant dry and brown. At first glance, before this test is made, one live and one dead plant may look almost identical, if the live one is completely dormant. Should you find that one branch of a tree or shrub is dead, do not assume that the entire plant is dead; try the test on several branches.

Sometimes, to the despair particularly of a new gardener, the leaves of his newly planted tree or shrub will come almost fully out and then, after a spell of hot, dry weather, the foliage will begin to wilt and dry up. But the plant will not necessarily die, though its future will depend largely on how fast you, the gardener, act.

Immediately you notice any general wilting and drying of foliage on a newly planted deciduous tree or shrub, remove all the affected growth before it has time to become completely dried up. That's right – pull off all the new leaves! If you act promptly, the plant will be prevented from losing any more moisture through transpiration, and will put out another set of leaves late in the season once its roots are capable of absorbing moisture.

Plants Really Can Be Permanent

In this chapter I have discussed many different species of trees and shrubs with the idea of having them live through the winter and be just as beautiful year after year as they were the first season they were planted.

To give your permanent plant a good start before winter approaches, give it that extra care to provide it with protection from the hard winter frosts. First, especially for evergreens planted on balconies, be certain that just before freeze-up the soil in your containers is well moistened. Also, if there is a slight thaw at any time during the winter, add a little more water to the soil. If possible, keep the containers with permanent plants out of the winter sun, regardless of what type of exposure they need during the growing season. In the winter, the sun adds to the hazards by causing plants (particularly evergreens) to lose water, but the frozen soil prevents it from being replaced. One final simple precaution to prevent excess water loss from the soil surface in winter as well as during the growing season: add an inch or two of chunky bark mulch, or a similar substance, to the tops of all your containers. A mulch not only slows down the water loss, it improves the look of your container plantings.

If, despite all your efforts, you are unsuccessful in growing trees and shrubs, more extreme protective measures may be necessary. Change to larger containers and place insulation along the bottom and sides before putting in the soil mix. Materials for insulation include polystyrene sheeting (the white foam trays, though not the cardboard, on which precut meats are sold form ideal insulating material at no cost), layers of foam rubber, fiberglas insulation sheeting, or even many layers of waxed corrugated cardboard. Any unwaxed paper product is likely to rot during the summer growing season, making it ineffective by winter. An additional protective layer of fiberglas could also be placed around the outside of the container. However, even in many northern cities, this added protection should not be necessary. Just go ahead with a weeping peashrub, or white spruce, or any of the others I have mentioned, taking the simpler precautions given earlier in this section, and in all probability you will have a permanent plant growing in a container on your balcony year after year.

7

Perennials, Roses, and Bulbs

Although trees, shrubs, and annuals may be all the garden that is required by some apartment dwellers, many others may wish to grow a wider variety of plants. Today, gardeners are growing selected perennials, roses, and bulbs on balconies, both in containers and in floor gardens, with the same optimism that they are growing trees and shrubs. Though the many colourful annuals remain indispensable, they are now no longer the only reliable splashes of colour recommended for balcony gardens.

Consider Vines

In Chapter 4, about annuals, I suggested a number of climbing plants that could be trained to grow up existing or improvised trellises on your balcony. With only a few exceptions, these twining or clinging plants are like the annual flowers and vegetables: they will live only for one season. But fortunately there are also some extremely hardy vines that grow in balcony containers and last from year to year.

Although it would be difficult for the large-flowering clematis (for example, hybrid varieties such as 'Jackmanii' and 'Nelly Moser' that are planted by so many ground-level gardeners) to live through the winters in an exposed container, they will be much more likely to survive if you insulate all sides of the container as described at the end of Chapter 6. However, there are two members of the clematis family that are considerably hardier than the large-flowered varieties and will survive container growth without any special protection in many climates: sweet autumn clematis (*Clematis paniculata*) and virgin's bower (*Clematis virginiana*). Both these vines are available from many garden centres, and although their flowers are not as large as those of the hybrids, both plants are interesting in their own right. Sweet autumn clematis is probably the prettier of the two, bearing a mass of small white flowers in late summer; the fragrance from the masses of bloom is very noticeable. In the autumn, silvery seed pods provide an eye-catching and colourful change from the more usual berries seen on most shrubs.

Many of the honeysuckles are vines, and show a wide variation in flower colour. Two in particular are hardy – the varieties early Dutch (*Lonicera* 'Early Dutch') and Dropmore scarlet (*Lonicera* 'Dropmore Scarlet'). Early Dutch produces a mass of pink buds which turn pale yellow and become fragrant as they open; Dropmore scarlet, as its name implies, has scarlet flowers – trumpet-shaped and nearly 2 inches long.

If you are looking for a vigorous, hardy vine and do not mind a non-flowering variety, you will probably find it difficult to improve on Virginia creeper (*Parthenocissus quinquefolia* 'Engelmannii'), which is hardy even in Regina and Saskatoon.

Unfortunately, there are very few evergreen vines. Some nurseries do offer a few varieties, but these do not seem to be reliably hardy

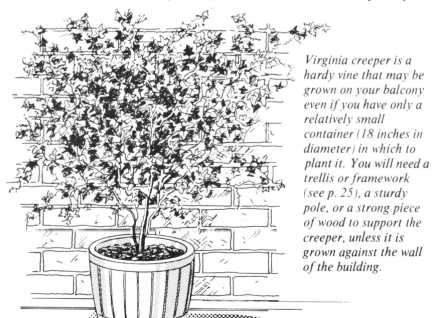

Virginia creeper is a hardy vine that may be grown on your balcony even if you have only a relatively small container (18 inches in diameter) in which to plant it. You will need a trellis or framework (see p. 25), a sturdy pole, or a strong piece of wood to support the creeper, unless it is grown against the wall of the building.

and are therefore not suitable for balcony containers unless you are prepared to insulate the containers for the winter months.

Few plants will give you such a genuine feeling of being in a real garden on your balcony as vines. But guard against planting too many of them, thus casting shade over your other plants. Vines should be planted in the same way as deciduous trees and shrubs; for planting instructions, see page 87. Since these more permanent vines are stronger growers than the annual varieties discussed in Chapter 4, you should use durable trellises, rather than light string, to support them.

Everyone Wants Roses

Leave a new gardener to his own devices in a garden centre or nursery, and you may be certain that one of the first plants he will select for his garden – balcony or not – will be a rose bush.

As anyone who has gardened at ground level knows, roses can be frustrating plants to grow. There seem to be many theories on their winter protection requirements, and yet, even in the mildest regions, few growers manage to bring all their bushes through every winter. There are always a few losses, and during a severe winter, up to a third of an amateur's ornamental roses may be wiped out. Because of the rose's basic lack of hardiness, it is obvious that rose bushes cannot be considered a permanent plant for balcony containers (except perhaps by the most ardent and patient enthusiasts), since the rose finds it so difficult to survive a typical Canadian winter.

One answer, though, for those who are determined to grow the Queen of Flowers on their balconies, is to plant new bushes each spring. While this may seem extravagant, if we remember that three good-quality rose bushes are still available for about the same price as one forty-ounce bottle of Scotch whisky, the price of a rose bush does not seem exorbitant. In fact, you are likely to remember the three months of bloom proffered by your rose bushes for far longer than the few days of cheer (depending on the number of friends you have) provided by the Scotch!

Of the three most popular groups of modern roses (hybrid teas, floribundas, and grandifloras), the balcony gardener would be wise to choose a medium- or low-growing bushy floribunda for his containers, since they will not exceed 3 feet in height. Hybrid tea and grandiflora varieties, which grow slightly taller, produce smaller numbers of larger flowers. Remember that a rose is really a shrub; its root system

How to plant a rose.

(1) Make a hole in the soil of your container large enough for the roots to be spread out. Prune off any bruised or broken roots. Set the bush in the hole so that the bump on its stem (called the 'bud union' – the place where the particular variety was grafted onto the rootstock) is an inch beneath the surface of the soil.

(2) Half fill the hole with soil, tamping it down carefully but firmly around the roots to make sure that no air pockets remain. Add about half a gallon of water, and wait until it disappears before filling the hole completely with soil and tamping it again.

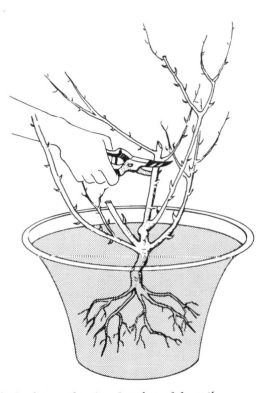

(3) Prune the bush to within 4 or 5 inches of the soil surface, making each cut just above a bud growth that is facing towards the outside of the bush. (If you have planted your rose very early and cannot see the buds, postpone the pruning until the buds appear.) Remove all spindly branches, leaving only 4 to 6 sturdy canes.

needs as much space as any deciduous shrub of the same height. Try not to select your roses just by choosing them from a catalogue: the colours shown are not always true to life, and only limited space is available for describing each rose. Go to your nearest nursery, garden centre, botanical garden, commercial rose field, or local rose show – *look*, and ask for information before you decide on which roses to plant. And, if you see a rose bush you particularly like growing in your area, find out its name from the owner or gardener and ask questions about it: how old is the bush? how tall will it be by the end of the season?

Roses need a sunny location and the same type of soil suggested for evergreens (p. 80). Since they are surface rooters, be sure to plant them in containers that are at least 24 inches wide, and unless you have a container larger than 48 inches wide, your roses will probably grow healthier root systems and show their blooms to better advantage if they are planted in separate containers rather than being crowded together. You should be able to plant them as soon as the soil is workable, when the largest and best selection of bushes is available from the grower. Give the bushes a liquid starter fertilizer (such as 10-45-15) right after you plant them; they should then be fertilized every three weeks with either a formula similar to 15-30-15 or the starter formula.

The roots of rose bushes do not like competition from other types of plants – especially from evergreens, shrubs, and strong-growing annual flowers such as petunias. If you wish, try a border of white sweet alyssum or lobelia around the edge of the container.

Another type of rose bush you may wish to consider for your outdoor containers is the miniature rose. These roses may be brought in from the balcony containers in September or October, before the first killing frost, and cut back severely for continuing growth indoors. Miniature roses indoors require plenty of light, and must therefore be placed either in a sunny window or, preferably, under deluxe cool white fluorescent tubes.

Flowers You Need Not Replant

Herbaceous perennials have for centuries been the mainstay of the flower garden, providing colour and dependable growth from year to year. These flowers die down to the ground each autumn and send up new stems again each spring. Delphiniums, irises, and peonies are, perhaps, the best examples. Though annual flowers are wonderful in providing an almost continuous display of colour from the time they are planted in May or June until the first heavy frost probably in October, they do have to be replanted each spring; herbaceous perennials do not.

During the 1960s, perennials as a whole suffered an acute decline in popularity, mainly because many new and superior varieties of colourful annuals were introduced and backed by substantial advertising and promotion. Now, as many gardeners search for alternatives to the usual petunias and marigolds, many of the perennials seem to be enjoying a new-found popularity. Though most perennials have a set blooming period of about a month, compared to a season-long blooming period for annuals, their spectacular flowers (for example, those of the delphinium) encourage many gardeners to attempt to grow them. As yet, little or no research has been carried out to tell us which of the herbaceous perennials will grow well in the balcony containers or floor gardens described in Chapter 3; we are left to our own devices in picking out only the hardiest species and trying them out in balcony containers.

From the hundreds of different herbaceous perennials available today, I have chosen only a dozen of those I consider to be the hardiest. All of them have been grown successfully in Kapuskasing, Ontario (zone 2), as well as in the same zone in other provinces, for example in Brandon, Manitoba; Rosthern, Saskatchewan; and Lacombe, Alberta. Most of the perennials I mention are fairly common and easily obtainable, but a few, such as false dragonhead and soapwort, are generally only available from better garden centres or reliable national mail-order nurseries.

Good drainage is essential for perennials, since their roots are subject to rot; to provide that, the containers in which they are planted should have at least one drainage hole. Most perennials need good humus material such as peat moss and sand (up to a third each by volume) and a regular application of liquid fertilizer once a month.

Among my first choices for a balcony perennial is the pearl sneezewort (*Achillea ptarmica* 'The Pearl'), which boasts masses of flat, white flower clusters in June and July. The 15-inch plants are a manageable size, and the flowers not only last well when cut, but may be easily dried for use through the winter in bouquets.

A fairly new selection, a variation of the well-known Carpathian harebell, has a long flowering season – from June to September. During that time, the 8-inch plants are almost covered with chalice-shaped blue flowers. This variety is blue carpet Carpathian harebell (*Campanula carpatica* 'Blue Carpet'). Growing to about the same height, the dwarf pinks, though they have a shorter flowering period (May to June), provide an extra bonus in that their red, pink, and white flowers are fragrant. These dwarf pinks are known by the botanical name *Dianthus plumarius* 'Nana'.

I think almost everyone knows snow-in-summer (*Cerastium tomentosum*), that creeping plant with silver-grey foliage often considered a weed in rock gardens because of its rapid rate of spreading growth. The 6-inch plants are covered with white flowers at the end of May, but the colour of the leaves is attractive throughout the season.

Baby's breath has long been a popular perennial with ground-level gardeners. Its many-branched, thin stems support thousands of tiny white flowers for nearly two months during July and August. One of the best of the double-flowering varieties is Bristol fairy baby's breath (*Gypsophila paniculata* 'Bristol Fairy'), which grows to a height of 30 inches. This is one of the plants for which good drainage and a sunny location are absolutely essential.

Irises are, perhaps, one of the most popular genera of herbaceous perennials. Though there are many varying types with diverse habits, I recommend that you try first the common tall bearded iris (*Iris pogoniris*) of which there are numerous varieties ranging in colour from white through pink, yellow, blue, mauve, and purple as well as interesting bi-colour combinations of these. Irises are one of the few plants that are best obtained and planted at a time of year other than spring. Early August is the time to divide iris rhizomes (the fleshy, almost bulbous roots), when your gardening friends may be quite willing to let you have prunings from the rhizomes of their more vigorous varieties for you to try in your containers. Be sure not to plant the rhizomes with more than an inch of soil over the top of the sharp-pointed growth buds.

Maltese cross (*Lychnis chalcedonica*) is an impressive and beautiful plant with large scarlet flower heads borne from mid-July to Sep-

After planting iris rhizomes an inch deep, cut back the foliage in a fan shape about 3 inches above the surface of the soil.

tember. Its height is 3 feet, and, like the oriental poppies suggested next, it is only suitable for containers that are 30 inches wide or more, in which shorter plants may be placed around the edge. Ideally, the Maltese cross could be surrounded with a contrasting perennial such as Carpathian harebell, which flowers at the same time, or with annual flowers such as petunias or yellow-gold marigolds, which grow to a maximum height of 18 to 20 inches.

Oriental poppies (*Papaver orientale*) are another favourite. When fully opened, their spectacular large blooms resemble a colourful patterned saucer. Colours of the many different varieties range from white through light pink, brilliant orange, crimson, scarlet, to deep mahogany. Some varieties produce double flowers. One problem presented by this plant, though, is that once the May to June flowering season is over, the foliage dies down to soil level, and you must be careful not to damage the roots when you put other plants into the same container. You might mark the position of the poppies with small stakes to remind you where they are. Remember that the suggestions for winter protection of herbaceous perennials that appear at the end of this chapter apply, of course, to the oriental poppies, even though they may have long been forgotten by the time the late autumn season arrives.

Perennial summer phlox (*Phlox paniculata*) shows beautiful multi-coloured bloom from early July into September. But in spite of the flowers, many amateur gardeners dislike the plant because during its blooming period it gradually loses all its bottom leaves, until all that remains is a spindly and ugly long stem. This loss of foliage is caused by the fast-spreading fungus disease powdery mildew, which fortunately is not as discouraging a problem as it once was, now that there is a systemic fungicide available to combat it. The colours of perennial summer phlox vary from white to dark purple and include brilliant scarlets and shocking pinks, along with numerous bi-colours. The plants like plenty of organic matter, so if you are replacing the soil after it has been in a container for two years or more, use plenty of leaf mould or dehydrated cattle manure in the new mixture. Liquid chemical fertilizer (15-30-15, or a similar analysis) should also be applied at least three times, twenty days apart, in the spring.

Not as well known as some of the plants I have already mentioned, yet worth trying as a container perennial, is false dragonhead (*Physostegia virginiana*). Vivid false dragonhead (*Physostegia virginiana* 'Vivid') is about the lowest-growing form, with a mature height of 24 inches. Its bright reddish-pink flowers on spikes appear in August and September. The curious shape of the petals more than rivals those of the annual snapdragon. False dragonhead needs sun in which to grow.

Another interesting herbaceous perennial, though less popular than false dragonhead, is soapwort (*Saponaria ocymoides*). Its masses of pink flowers completely cover its trailing foliage during June. Finally, the spike speedwell (*Veronica spicata*), a slender plant 24 inches in height, might well be tried. Bearing thin, pointed spikes of deep-bluish violet flowers, this plant shows its colours from July to the first frost in the fall. Like the perennial summer phlox, it is one of many different species within the same genus, but is the most reliable for experimentation in balcony containers.

The young growth of taller-growing herbaceous perennials such as summer phlox, Maltese cross, false dragonhead, and spike speedwell will respond well to pinching in late spring up to the middle of June. Pinching will give bushier plants and more flowers.

Winter Protection of Herbaceous Perennials

On the subject of winter protection, I suggest that you first read the general suggestions at the end of Chapter 6 for protecting containers of permanent plants. In addition to those suggestions, there are a few special methods that can help to protect your herbaceous perennials. These will have a much better chance of survival if the top and sides of the containers are covered over with dry straw for the winter, though this should not be done until the soil has completely frozen in late fall. If you prefer not to use straw, Christmas tree branches make an excellent substitute provided they are spread as early in January as possible. However, if you live in a part of the country where winter has really begun by early November, it would be foolish to wait until January to cover the containers with Christmas trees, for the frost will probably already have killed some of your plants. Other types of covering include insulation batts obtainable from local building supply stores, or several layers of corrugated cardboard from the boxes discarded by supermarkets, and so on. Plastic film or polyethylene should not be used. Cut off the dead tops of the plants a few inches above soil level, then place your insulation material over and around the containers.

Regardless of the amount of light needed by any of the herbaceous perennials – be it sun or shade – during the winter the covered containers should be kept in the shade if at all possible. Shade will help to prevent the very damaging effects of the alternate freezing and thawing that occurs when cold nights are followed by sunny days.

Spring-flowering Bulbs on the Balcony

Although many bulb dealers have insisted that spring-flowering bulbs will not thrive outdoors in containers, several members of the Highrise Gardeners of Toronto club have grown various kinds of bulbs successfully on their balconies. Since no particular varieties of bulbs are hardier than any others, the problems of growing them cannot be overcome in the same way that I suggested for evergreens, trees, shrubs, and vines, by choosing especially hardy varieties. Instead, attention should be focused on methods of protecting the containers from the extremes of winter temperatures – a course of action pursued by the keen Highrise Gardeners club members. They plant their bulbs in a portable foam cooler, which they protect on all sides, as well as on the top and bottom, with double layers of fiberglas insulation sheeting.

Because I know it may be difficult to drill holes through containers made of metal or concrete, I have not insisted that the bulb containers have holes at the bottom – therefore space for drainage is more important. However, if you are using containers that have no drainage holes, be careful not to water the soil to such an extent that the drainage space eventually fills up.

The bulbs should be planted at the normal planting time, from about the middle of October to November in southern Ontario and areas with similar climates. If you are planting daffodils or narcissi, the earlier in the autumn these are planted the better the results will be. After the container for the bulbs has been chosen (the insulated soft-drink cooler is ideal) choose a soil mix suited to bulbs. Commercial mixes for this purpose are available, but it is best to mix your own, using a third each of good garden soil, peat moss, and perlite. Be sure to obtain sufficient drainage material (large gravel, small stones, or rubble) and include some charcoal in chunks. Put this material at the bottom of the container to a depth of at least a fifth of its total depth. If the drainage material is extremely coarse and the soil mix is likely to fill all the crevices between it, put a sheet of burlap, an old piece of window screening, or even a length of porous cloth over the top of the drainage material before putting in the soil mix in order to retain the drainage space at the bottom of the container.

The method of planting bulbs in containers closely resembles that of planting them in the ground. First, put about 3 inches of soil mix into the container on top of the drainage material and firm it down. Then place the bulbs quite close together and add additional soil mix to cover them to almost twice their depth. As you add the soil, it should be firmed between, around, and over the bulbs. If you follow these suggestions, you should find that a few inches of space have been left between the soil level and the top of the container, in which the bulbs may grow before the lid is removed in the spring.

It is very important that bulbs in outside containers not be allowed to dry out. This is not as simple as it sounds, since you should wrap up the containers with insulation sheeting after having planted the bulbs. It is a good idea to keep this need for moisture in mind when you wrap the containers with double layers of fiberglas insulation. Secure the lid separately, so that you can remove it easily periodically to check the moisture and in early spring to watch for the first green shoots.

Once you have begun to grow bulbs in containers, you will doubtless be able to devise your own successful tricks that may improve or simplify the procedure for you. Use your imagination!

8

Some Balcony Extras

Flourishing green plants, with or without colourful blooms, are the essence of your balcony garden, and may also be all that you require for your garden off the ground. But some gardeners will want to add still more beauty and interest to their balconies by including artificial turf, a fountain, or lighting – and all gardeners should consider treating their house plants to a summer out-of-doors, as a change from their usual indoor habitat.

Turf Grows Up

It is often said of ground-level gardening that the good lawn creates the garden – in other words, that an expanse of neatly trimmed lawn properly sets off a colourful flower or shrub border. While it is not impossible to grow some turf on larger balconies, it is impractical and would require an unwarranted amount of time as well as a considerable financial investment.

Until recently, the only available substitute for turf on a balcony was the usual green indoor-outdoor carpet – but now, if you do not wish to use carpet and want a lawn on your balcony, there is an alternative. Try artificial turf, that synthetic more grass-like than grass product which provides the surface of many fields used for professional sport. It is now made by a number of different manufacturers, and is available through a wide variety of retail outlets and even by mail through mail-order houses. Cut to the exact dimensions of your balcony, artificial turf will give your high-rise outdoor living area a totally new aura. You may set your containers directly on it, or on casters (as suggested in Chapter 3) that are designed to roll on carpet. If you choose to have a floor garden, you should cut the artificial turf so that it fits right up against the side boards of the floor garden, in that way creating a garden as closely resembling an authentic ground-level garden as possible, if that is your goal.

When you are considering the purchase of artificial turf, be sure to look at as many different types as possible; wide variations in simulated grass products are available, and you should be able to find one that really appeals to you. A word of caution, which applies both to artificial turf and to indoor-outdoor carpeting: cigarette butts smouldering even very slightly on the floor are the greatest enemy of these floor coverings; therefore, if smokers are using your balcony, provide ashtrays and impress upon them that they absolutely must avoid dropping their butts on your 'lawn'.

A fiberglas rock cascade is economical, and an ideal way of adding interest to your balcony.

Water Adds Movement

A feature that ambitious balcony gardeners may want to add to their high-rise gardens is a fountain or water cascade, for water really does add new life and movement to any garden. Complete kits for small fountains are now available, most of them designed to build a fountain that will fit into a 30-inch or larger balcony container. The only requirements are sufficient space and a source of electric current – probably an extension cord brought outside through perhaps either a low window or a sliding doorway. Building managers may be sympathetic in helping or at least allowing the semi-permanent installation of the cord through a door or window casement.

One of the most attractive and compact arrangements I have seen is an artificial water cascade (really just a trickle of water) falling over rocks made of fiberglas. A unit such as this could be set in a corner of a balcony among a small planting of annual flowers to provide interest throughout the summer months. Drained of water in the winter, it may be left outside without cracking or breaking.

Lighting the Night

One of the interesting and particularly effective mechanical additions to a balcony garden is night lighting. But most apartment gardeners will sigh with frustration at the thought of lighting their gardens, because they know they will be faced with the same problem I mentioned had to be overcome in installing fountains – the lack of an electrical outlet on the balcony. This shortcoming may gradually be overcome as apartment developers and builders begin to include balcony outlets, but if you live in an older building and are without an outlet, there is an alternative. Although most garden light fixtures are the usual 110-volt equipment, some of the newer ones are built to operate on low-voltage systems similar to the systems that operate electric trains or door buzzers. The advantage is that the lights work off a transformer which can be plugged into an outlet inside the apartment. The low-voltage power lines (safer than 110-volt lines) that are used to carry the electricity out onto the balcony then need only be very thin, and are much more easily inserted through a door or window opening than the larger lines.

Lighting your balcony at night will turn it into an illuminated magic area for evening entertaining. And, since the lighting fixtures are movable, you can set them anywhere you like to accent different containers or planting arrangements according to the season.

House Plants: A Change

The final addition I want to suggest for your balcony garden is a group of decorative plants that you may already be growing but have overlooked as assets to your balcony – your indoor or house plants. Most of the potted ivies, geraniums, and the various foliage plants will grow well on a balcony during the summer months. If you like a number of large plants such as palms, dracaenas, dumbcanes, and ferns in your apartment to provide a more livable environment, you may not have considered moving them outside to your balcony as the basis for a tropical setting during the summer. But keep in mind that if your balcony faces south, west, or southwest, and has no provision for shade, then it would probably be best to leave your indoor plants inside, for outdoors they will be burned by the sun. However, if your balcony faces east or north, your large indoor plants should thrive outdoors from mid-June to mid-September. Plants such as palms, philodendrons, treebine begonia (*Cissus discolor*), and croton will flourish, though you will have to water them more often than if they were indoors.

Regardless of the schedule for fertilizing your indoor plants when they are inside, they should receive a monthly application of liquid fertilizer (with a formula such as 25-15-20 for foliage plants, or 15-30-15 for flowering plants) while they are out-of-doors. During their summer outside, you may notice some of the green leaves turning bronze, a change probably caused by the sudden exposure to a much greater amount of light – sun in particular. Usually, only some of the older leaves are affected, a loss easily offset by the new growths produced in response to the better growing conditions outside.

Just before you move your plants indoors again in September, spray them thoroughly with an insecticide such as malathion, or a house plant spray, for they are more likely to become infested by insects while outside. In addition, the lower stems of palms and other large plants should be examined for clusters of scale insects, which resemble tiny round fish scales. To remove these, dip a discarded toothbrush into correctly diluted insecticide and brush them off, perhaps into an empty jar or can. Your house plants should then be ready to perform at their best throughout the winter months.

9

Insect and Disease Control

'The optimist who said insects do not go above the eighth floor has never lived on the tenth,' claimed a tenth-floor apartment gardener whose efforts had all but been wiped out by the pest known as greenhouse white fly. He was right – nor could the optimist have risen higher, or he might have seen insect-infested balcony gardens even on the twentieth floors of modern high-rise buildings.

Steps to Eliminate Pests and Diseases

Prevention of insect infestations and diseases begins for apartment gardens at the same time as it does for ground-level gardens, though it is a time when neither group of gardeners is thinking of taking such action, let alone prepared to act. Early or mid-March is the time to apply a dormant oil spray to all the containers you used in previous years. At the same time, it won't hurt to spray in the corners and along the crevices of the balcony, too, places where many insect pests winter in a dormant state; the spray applied early will kill them at this harmless stage. Dormant oil sprays, like all the other products for the control of insects and diseases mentioned in this chapter, are obtainable from your local garden centre, the garden shops of major department stores, and from most mail-order seed houses and nurseries.

Since modern architecture decrees that apartment balconies (and, therefore, apartment gardens) are to exist in relative isolation, pest and disease control is somewhat simpler than for ground-level gardens. Because of this isolation, there is a second step that you may take to guard your plants against infestation – though this step becomes less effective if the balconies surrounding yours are also used for gardening. Put every new seedling or purchased plant somewhere in your apartment away from all other plants for about ten days. As an alternative, give all your newly acquired plants a protective spraying with a good general-purpose insecticide, such as malathion. Any insect on a plant should either become visible in the ten-day isolation period or be killed by the preventive spray. The third step is to use only sterilized soil mixes, or to buy or mix your own lightweight (sterile) medium, as explained in Chapter 2 (page 13). If you follow these three suggestions, you should have no major problems with insects and diseases.

If you already have an established balcony garden, and your plants are being attacked by pests or diseases, then you should consider the three preventive measures for next year, following the suggestions in this section.

Insects and Other Pests

Even after you have taken these general precautions, you may find yourself playing host to unwanted insect guests and in need of information on how to eliminate them. There are several ways of getting rid of these pests – the most successful is still to spray them with the appropriate insecticides. Biological controls have received much publicity recently, but they are still a long way from being completely effective. Various predator insects, including the harmless insect-eating ladybird beetle or ladybug, may be purchased in quantities, but often – particularly on a balcony – they turn out to be as great a nuisance as the original pest, even if they don't fly away before doing their job. Planting certain plants (chives, for instance) is said to dispel insects from the general vicinity, but in fact even a small balcony would need so many chive plants that there would be little space left for flowers and vegetables.

The most common insect pests on balconies are aphids (known also as green fly), soft-bodied flies, averaging an eighth of an inch in length, which may be green, red, or black. They cluster on flower stems and suck the plants' sap, eventually weakening them severely. Almost as common as aphids are white flies, sometimes known as greenhouse white flies. These are tiny sucking insects that are difficult to observe unless the foliage of their host plants (fuchsia, ageratum, and lantana are particularly susceptible) is disturbed. The white flies then take wing, only to settle again almost immediately. They cause some leaves to turn yellow, but until the infestation is severe, damage from the flies is minimal – they are more of a nuisance than anything else. The honeydew produced by these white flies (specks of sticky plant sap) often covers any type of surface adjacent to the plants. Since white flies hatch out every few days, you should use a spray at least as often as that to get rid of each infestation.

To get rid of aphids and white flies, an insecticide such as malathion, or one of the systemic insecticides, is the best to use on most plants – except petunias and African violets, and remember that vegetables should not be subjected to a systemic insecticide. However, malathion will only suppress white flies if it is applied regularly every two days. Aphids are easier to control: one or two applications in a week should be enough. Be sure to follow the manufacturer's directions on the label.

Other common pests are leafhoppers – small, sucking insects that jump when disturbed; tarnished plant bugs – shiny, wingless beetles a quarter of an inch long, which cause deformed flowers; mites, which are almost invisible, but cause foliage to turn yellow or grey and usually deposit a fine, silk-like webbing on the leaves; and various scale insects which appear on the stems of plants as motionless, flaky protrusions resembling fish scales. All these insects may be successfully treated with malathion, though some types of mite tend to be resistent to it, and you should use a stronger miticide.

Occasionally, cutworms, slugs, or snails may be living in the soil around plants you have just purchased. While cutworms can be killed with insecticides, it is usually best to protect newly planted seedlings or young plants with bands of cardboard extending 2 inches above the soil level. These bands will prevent the cutworms from severing the tender young plants just above ground level. Slugs, though a major problem in some ground-level gardens, should not be a major concern on balconies. If you do see them, or their typical damage – chewed flowers, fruit or foliage, especially if the leaves are touching the soil – it is usually easiest to pick them off at night, by hand, when they are active. If you must use a chemical for a slug infestation, you will find a special bait material containing metaldehyde at garden supply shops. But try prevention first: beware the unstaked tomato plant, which will attract slugs.

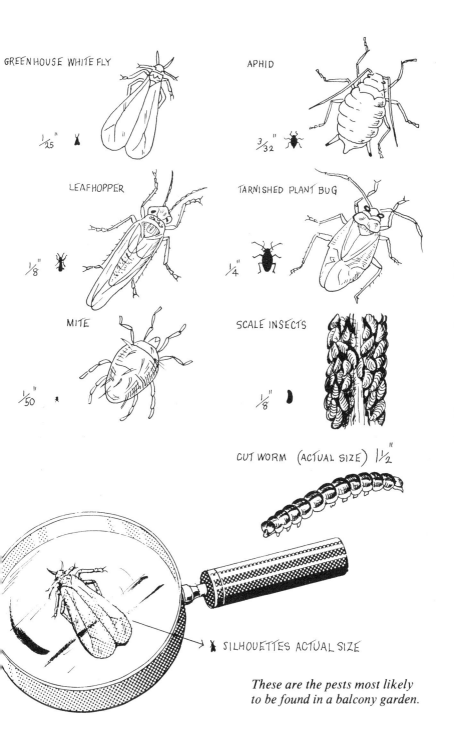

GREENHOUSE WHITE FLY

$\frac{1}{25}$"

APHID

$\frac{3}{32}$"

LEAFHOPPER

$\frac{1}{8}$"

TARNISHED PLANT BUG

$\frac{1}{4}$"

MITE

$\frac{1}{50}$"

SCALE INSECTS

$\frac{1}{8}$"

CUT WORM (ACTUAL SIZE) $1\frac{1}{2}$"

SILHOUETTES ACTUAL SIZE

These are the pests most likely to be found in a balcony garden.

Many of the insects referred to in this section may occur on vegetables. If they do, be doubly cautious in reading and understanding the directions on the label before applying any insecticide. For most vegetables, a waiting period of from three to five days is necessary from the time of the last application of insecticide to harvest. Bear in mind that systemic insecticides are not to be applied at all to vegetables.

The best source of information on up-to-date chemical controls for insects is your provincial department of agriculture; alternative sources are the major insecticide manufacturers – each one publishes annually an excellent illustrated booklet on sensible pest control which is available free on request.

Plant Diseases

Unless you grow plants such as roses, phlox, and tuberous begonias, which are particularly susceptible to diseases, these should be of even less concern to you than the insect pests. The most annoying and disappointing will probably be 'damping off', a common disease that causes newly germinated seedlings to rot at soil level. It may be prevented by using only sterilized soil or other sterile medium for starting seeds, and by dusting the seed with captan or thiram fungicide before you sow it.

Powdery mildew (a white fungus growth on the surface of the upper leaves), black spot (circular black spots on the leaves), botrytis blight (tiny water-soaked spots on the flowers and foliage), and leaf spot (enlarging spots on the leaves) are four other common plant diseases that are all easier to prevent than cure. The following three precautions will be a great help in preventing a large number of plant diseases in addition to the ones I have just mentioned. Do not leave dead flowers or foliage to rot on the soil, do not overcrowd your containers, and be sure to discard immediately any infected plant parts. If a disease does reach your balcony, fungicides such as captan, sulphur, dinocap, and zineb, or a combination of fungicides, all available from garden supply dealers, should help to solve the problem. Look, too, for the new systemic fungicides, which last longer than the older types and are particularly effective against powdery mildew.

Whether you are a new gardener, or one who has gardened for years at ground level and has recently joined the thousands of balcony gardeners, you will doubtless encounter some unusual problem or pest. Pigeons, for instance, can often be a nuisance, and the best methods of control are probably strictly mechanical: frightening them away (try strips of aluminum strung on wires) and eliminating their roosting spots, perhaps by fencing them off with chicken wire. If you have a particular problem that seems unique, consult one of the sources beginning on page 113. If possible, rather than telephoning take the 'sick' plant, or a sample of the problem, to the gardening authority. Should one source be unable to help you, be sure to ask where you might go for an answer to your question.

Sources for Information and Problem Solving

General Sources

Chevron Chemical Canada Ltd., Ortho Division, 1016 Industry Street, Oakville, Ontario, L6J 2X4.

> Publishers of the comprehensive *Lawn and Garden Book*, with annual revisions, detailing pest control and giving other gardening hints; available from leading garden supply dealers or direct from the company.

Chipman Chemicals Ltd., P.O. Box 9100, Stoney Creek, Ontario, L8G 3Y4.

> Publishers of Flip Chart Spray Calendar, revised annually, showing proper sprays for insects and diseases; available direct from the company and authorized dealers.

FMC Canada Ltd., Agricultural Chemical Division; offices in all major cities. Main office: Burlington, Ontario, L7S 1W6.

> Publishers of illustrated brochures on various phases of gardening, available from the company's dealers or local offices.

Green Cross Products, a division of Ciba-Geigy Canada Ltd.; offices in Moncton, Montreal, Toronto, and Winnipeg. Main office: 1 Westside Drive, Islington, Ontario, M9C 1B2.

> Publishers of garden care folder with information on insect and disease control, available from dealers and company offices.

Ornamental Research Service, Agriculture Canada, Central Experimental Farm, Ottawa, Ontario, K1A 0C5. *Attention/Att.* Director.

> Technical and research services, plant identification, information pamphlets (from the Information Division), greenhouses, 98-acre display grounds of all types of hardy plants.

Ornamentals Section, Morden Research Station, Agriculture Canada, Morden, Manitoba, R0G 1J0. *Att.* Head of Ornamentals.

> Technical and research services, plant identification and display grounds of reliably hardy plants.

Provincial Sources

ALBERTA

Alberta Horticultural Association, c/o Mrs. Frank Adamson, Corresponding Secretary, Lacombe, Alberta, T0C 1S0.

> The provincially funded parent association for the local horticultural societies in many cities and towns in Alberta. Members are amateur gardeners. Holds annual convention.

Botanic Garden, Department of Botany, The University of Alberta, Edmonton, Alberta, T6G 2E1. *Att.* Director.

> Newly established botanic garden located ten miles southwest of Edmonton, comprising just under 100 acres of plant trials, especially perennials hardy in northern Alberta climate. Has active members' organization. Publishes seed list and a bulletin twice a year.

Calgary Parks/Recreation Department, P.O. Box 2100, Calgary, Alberta, T2P 2M5. *Att.* Horticultural Extension Officer.

> Gardening advice, plant identification, problem solving, and gardening lectures, supplied through the resources of the parks department.

BRITISH COLUMBIA

British Columbia Council of Garden Clubs, c/o Mrs. Joyce Goodman, Corresponding Secretary, 862 Shasta Crescent, Coquitlam, British Columbia, V3J 6G3.

> Parent association of over twenty garden clubs, societies, and specialized plant societies operating in many areas of the province. Most of the members are amateur gardeners.

Botanical Gardens, University of British Columbia, Vancouver, British Columbia, V6T 1W5. *Att.* Education Co-ordinator or Director.

> A developing botanic garden with significant resources including greenhouses, specialized gardens, research facilities; courses for amateurs on plant identification and problem solving.

Van Dusen Botanical Gardens, 37th and Oak Street, Vancouver, British Columbia. *Att.* Curator.

> A botanical display garden together with membership organization located in the centre of the city; courses and seminars, displays of popular plants; problem solving and plant identification. Open membership.

MANITOBA

Manitoba Horticultural Association, c/o Manitoba Department of Agriculture, 908 Norquay Building, Winnipeg, Manitoba, R3C 0P8. *Att.* Secretary.

> The provincially funded parent association for horticultural societies in Winnipeg and small communities throughout Manitoba. Membership is primarily of amateur gardeners.

NEW BRUNSWICK

Fredericton Garden Club, c/o Dr. Dorothy Farmer, 165 Liverpool Street, Fredericton, New Brunswick, E3B 4V6.

> The largest garden club in the province. Most of the members are amateur gardeners.

NEWFOUNDLAND

Newfoundland Horticultural Society, P.O. Box 1033, St. John's, Newfoundland, A1C 5M3.

> Amateur gardeners and some professionals meet monthly in this society. It holds an annual flower show in August. Open membership.

NOVA SCOTIA

Nova Scotia Association of Garden Clubs, c/o Mrs. J. J. Holmes, Secretary, 17 Cameron Street, Dartmouth, Nova Scotia, B2Y 2G7.

> Parent association of over forty clubs, partially provincially funded, with more than 1500 amateur and semi-professional members.

Arboretum and Horticultural Science Department, Ontario Agricultural College, University of Guelph, Guelph, Ontario, N1G 2W1.

Technical and research services, plant identification, private library, greenhouses, display grounds of some types of plants, 240-acre arboretum, and gardening lectures for the amateur.

Civic Garden Centre, Edwards Gardens, 777 Lawrence Avenue East, Don Mills, Ontario, M3C 1P2. *Att.* Executive Director.

Located within a 46-acre garden park with displays of various types of plants. Open membership, affiliated specialized clubs, members' meetings, courses and lectures, garden lending library, plant identification, technical services, garden supply and book shops. Publishes the gardening magazine *Trellis.*

Highrise Gardeners of Toronto, c/o Civic Garden Centre, Edwards Gardens, 777 Lawrence Avenue East, Don Mills, Ontario, M3C 1P2.

Club with open membership, affiliated with the non-profit Civic Garden Centre; meets monthly to hear speakers; publishes monthly bulletin; has use of extensive gardening library.

Horticultural Research Institute, Ontario Ministry of Agriculture and Food, Vineland Station, Ontario, L0R 2E0. *Att.* Director.

Technical and research services, plant identification, display grounds of some types of plants, and insect laboratory.

The Niagara Parks Commission, School of Horticulture, P.O. Box 150, Niagara Falls, Ontario, L2E 6T2. *Att.* Superintendent.

Technical services, plant identification, private library, greenhouses, 100-acre display grounds of many types of plants.

Ontario Horticultural Association, c/o Ontario Ministry of Agriculture and Food, Parliament Buildings, Queen's Park, Toronto, Ontario, M7A 1A3. *Att.* Secretary.

Parent association for approximately 250 individual horticultural societies which receive provincial grants and are located in small and large communities throughout the province. Most of the members are amateur gardeners. The association holds an annual convention.

Royal Botanical Gardens, P.O. Box 399, Hamilton, Ontario, L8N 3H8. *Att.* Director.

> Open membership. Courses and lectures, plant identification, 1900-acre display grounds with thousands of species of plants; greenhouses, gardening library, technical and research services. Publishes *The Garden's Bulletin* and a newsletter for members.

PRINCE EDWARD ISLAND

Prince Edward Island Rural Beautification Society, c/o Mr. Keith L. Brehaut, Bunbury Nursery, P.O. Box 70, Charlottetown, P.E.I., C1A 7K2.

> Open membership society with the aim of planting trees and shrubs throughout the province to enhance its beauty.

QUEBEC

Montreal Botanical Gardens, 4101 Sherbrooke Street East, Montreal, P.Q., H1X 2B2. *Att.* Director.

> Technical and research services, greenhouses, 190-acre display grounds of hardy plants, courses and lectures for amateur gardeners, and plant and pest identification.

Morgan Arboretum, Macdonald College, McGill University, P.O. Box 500, Ste Anne de Bellevue, P.Q., H9X 3L6.

> Technical services and a 700-acre arboretum of native trees and shrubs.

Provincial Council of Horticultural Societies of Quebec, c/o Mr. E. B. Jubien, Secretary, 150 Vivian Avenue, Town of Mount Royal, P.Q., H3P 1N7.

> A nucleus of horticultural societies from some communities; not provincially funded. Members are primarily amateur gardeners.

Technical Institute of Agriculture, P.O. Box 40, St. Hyacinthe, P.Q., J2S 7B2. *Att.* Agronomist.

> Technical and research services, plant identification, pest information, and advice for amateurs.

SASKATCHEWAN

Saskatchewan Horticultural Association, c/o Extension Division, University of Saskatchewan, Saskatoon, Saskatchewan, S7N 0W0. *Att.* Secretary.

Parent association of horticultural societies in various communities in Saskatchewan, partially provincially funded. Most members are amateur gardeners.

ALL PROVINCES

In addition to the organizations listed here, each province has a ministry or department of agriculture which publishes pamphlets and informative booklets on various phases of gardening. Contact the appropriate agency through the legislative buildings in the capital city of your province for detailed information on the resources available.

Seeds and Sundries

Dominion Seed House, Georgetown, Ontario, L7G 4A2.

W. H. Perron and Co. Ltd., 515 Labelle Blvd., Chomedey (Laval), P.Q.

Stokes Seeds, Ltd., 39 James Street, St. Catharines, Ontario, L2R 6R6.

T. & T. Seeds, Ltd., 120 Lombard Avenue, Winnipeg, Manitoba, R3B 0W3.

Bibliography

A selection of gardening books for reference.

Abraham, George, *Raise Vegetables Without a Garden* (Barrington, Illinois; Countryside Books, 1974) 80 pp., paperback; many sketches. Growing vegetables in containers.

Baylis, Maggie, *House Plants for the Purple Thumb* (San Francisco; 101 Productions, 1973) 192 pp.; excellent sketches of plants and indoor gardening techniques.

Cherry, Elaine C., *Fluorescent Light Gardening* (New York; Van Nostrand Reinhold, 1965) 256 pp.; sketches and some black-and-white photographs.

Crockett, James Underwood, *Flowering House Plants* (New York; Time-Life, 1971) 160 pp; illustrated in full colour. An encyclopaedia of these plants and their care.

Crockett, James Underwood, *Foliage House Plants* (New York; Time-Life, 1971) 160 pp; illustrated in full colour. An encyclopaedia of these plants and their care.

Dale, H. Fred, *Fred Dale's Garden Book* (Toronto; General Publishing, 1973) 198 pp., paperback; black-and-white photographs.

Elbert, George A. and Virginie, *Fun with Terrarium Gardening* (New York; Crown Publishers, 1973) 144 pp., available in paperback; many sketches and photographs, including some in colour.

Elbert, George A., *The Indoor Light Gardening Book* (New York; Crown Publishers, 1973) 250 pp.; colour and black-and-white photographs, also sketches, throughout.

Fletcher, H. L. V., *Gardening in Window Boxes and Other Containers* (London, England; Pelham Books, 1969) 159 pp.; black-and-white photographs.

Herwig, Rob, *128 Houseplants You Can Grow* (New York; Macmillan, 1972) 60 pp., paperback; 128 full-colour illustrations, an excellent identification guide.

Kranz, Frederick H. and Jacqueline L., *Gardening Indoors Under Lights* (New York; Viking Press, 1971) 242 pp.; sketches and some black-and-white photographs.

Loewer, H. Peter, *The Indoor Water Gardener's How-To Handbook* (New York; Walker, 1965) 96 pp.; many sketches of plants and of water gardening techniques.

McDonald, Elvin, *The Complete Book of Gardening Under Lights* (New York; Doubleday, 1965) 215 pp., available in paperback; a few black-and-white photographs and sketches.

Perper, Hazel, *The Avocado Pit Growers Indoor How-to Book* (New York; Walker, 1965) 63 pp.; sketches of techniques. Growing avocados indoors.

Skelsey, Alice, *Cucumbers in a Flowerpot* (New York; Workman, 1971) 87 pp.; many black-and-white sketches. How to grow vegetables in containers.

Taloumis, George, *Container Gardening Outdoors* (New York; Simon and Schuster, 1972) 95 pp.; well illustrated with colour and black-and-white photographs.

Taloumis, George, *Outdoor Gardening in Pots and Boxes* (New York; Van Nostrand Reinhold, 1962) 235 pp.; colour and black-and-white photographs.

Teusher, Henry, *Window-Box Gardening* (New York; Macmillan, 1956) 180 pp.; illustrated with some black-and-white photographs.

Wilson, Lois, *Chatelaine's Gardening Book* (Toronto; Maclean-Hunter, 1970) 369 pp.; profusely illustrated in colour and black-and-white, also sketches of plants and techniques.

Index

Main references in bold type.
References to illustrations in italics.

P

Pachystima, 78
Palms, 105
Papaver, 98
Patience plant, 46
Peaches, 65
Peas, 64
Peashrub
—cutleaf, 87
—globe Siberian, 84
—Siberian, 74
—weeping, **74**, 75, 82
Peat moss, 13, **23**, 33, 47, 51, 68,
  81, 96, 100
Perennial flowers
—suitable types, 96-9
—winter protection, 99
Perlite, 47, 51, 54, 58, 68, 100
Petunias, 10, 17, 25, **37-9**, *38*, 40,
  52, 54, 56, 95, 98, 108
Philodendron, 13
Phlox, perennial summer, **98**, 99,
  110
Phosphorus (phosphate), **13**, 70
Physocarpus, 85
Physostegia, 96, **98**
Picea, 76, 79-80
Pigeons, 110
Pine
—bristlecone, 78
—dwarf Scots, 79
—mugho, 77, *78*
—Swiss stone, 80
Pinks, dwarf, 96
Pinus, 77, *78*, 79, 80
Plant Hardiness Zone Map, 72-3
Poppies, oriental, 98
Portulaca, **40-1**, 66
Potassium nitrate, 12-13
Potash, 14
Potentilla, 87

Pothos, 31
Powdery mildew, 98, **110**
Prunus, **83**, 86
Pueraria, 46

R

Radishes, **61**, 66
Rhus, 86
Rock cascade, *103*, 104
Rose daphne, 78
Roses
—diseases, 110
—ideal type, 93
—locations for, 95
—miniature varieties, 95
—planting of, *94*, 95
Russian olive, 85

S

Saltpetre, 12-13
Salvia, **42**, 43
Sand, 47, 51, 54, 58, 68, 96
Santolina, 44
Saponaria, 99
Saskatoon berry, 83, 86
Scale insects, 105, 108, *109*
Scarlet runner beans, 46
Sea-buckthorn, 85
Self-watering containers, 11, **23-5**,
  24
Shepherdia, 85
Shrubs
—deciduous, 84-7
—evergreen, 75-80
—planting of, 80-1, 87-8, *88*
Slugs, 108
Snails, 108
Snapdragons, 10, 27, *41*, **42**, 52, 56
Sneezewort, pearl, 96
Snowball, European, *84*
Snow-in-summer, 97
Soapwort, 96, **99**

This book is set in 10/12 New Times Roman, with
captions in 10/11 italics; chapter titles in Goudy Catalogue;
subheadings in 11 pt New Times Roman italics.
The stock is 60 lb Concorde.

1 2 3 4 5 6 7 8 9 10 WO 84 83 82 81 80 79 78 77 76 75